SELECTED WRITINGS OF
CHARLES OLSON

SELECTED WRITINGS
OF
CHARLES OLSON

Edited, with an Introduction, by
ROBERT CREELEY

NEW DIRECTIONS

Published simultaneously in Canada
by George J. McLeod, Ltd, Toronto

Manufactured in the United States of America.

New Directions Books are published for James Laughlin
by New Directions Publishing Corporation,
80 Eighth Avenue, New York 10011

NINTH PRINTING

Acknowledgments are gratefully made to the following, for permission to reprint the material here included:

PART I

to the Auerhahn Society, for material from *Human Universe* (San Francisco, 1965);

PART II

to the Divers Press, for the text of *Mayan Letters* (Mallorca, 1953);

PART III

to the Auerhahn Society, for material from *Human Universe* (San Francisco, 1965);

PART IV

to Caresse Crosby, the Black Sun Press, for material from *y & x* (Washington, 1948);
to Cid Corman, Origin Press, for material from *In Cold Hell, In Thicket* (Dorchester, Massachusetts, 1953);
and to Grove Press, for material from *The Distances* (New York, 1960);

PART V

to Jonathan Williams and Ted and Eli Wilentz, Jargon Books in association with Corinth Books, Inc. (New York, 1960).

He left him naked,
the man said, and
nakedness
is what one means

that all start up
to the eye and soul
as though it had never
happened before

Maximus, to Gloucester
Letter 27

CONTENTS

INTRODUCTION

1

It is simple enough to note the main details of Charles Olson's background. Born December 27, 1910, he lived for a time in Worcester, Massachusetts, but then his family moved while he was still quite young to Gloucester, on the coast of the same state. I once saw a picture of him, aged about eleven, taken together with the whole community of Dogtown at that time, some twenty people who lived in this part of Gloucester, separated from the main town by the Cut or channel that runs in to the inner harbor. He is sitting on the edge of a roof and his legs hang down very evidently, giving a sense of the size he will later have as a man. He was to be tall indeed, roughly six foot eight or nine.

Subsequently he went first to Wesleyan, then to Yale and Harvard, and got a Ph. D. in American Studies from the latter. His jobs were various. He worked on a fishing boat, he was a mailman for awhile in Gloucester, he taught at Clark and Harvard for relatively brief periods, he was chairman to foreign language groups for the Democratic Party during Roosevelt's campaign for a fourth term. Then, in the late forties, he took a job vacated by Edward Dahlberg, at that point a close and significant friend, to teach at Black Mountain College in North Carolina on the invitation of Josef Albers, then rector of the college. Albers soon after went to Yale, and in the early fifties Olson became rector. Although it was a difficult time financially for all involved, and the college had relatively few students, nonetheless Black Mountain proved a focal point for much significant activity in the arts. John Cage, Robert Duncan, Merce Cunningham, Franz Kline—all of whom were present at one time or another during this period—show briefly the range and intensity of what was then happening. The students —John Weiners, Robert Rauschenberg, Edward Dorn, John Chamberlain, Michael Rumaker, Cy Twombley, Joel Oppenheimer, Dan Rice, Fielding Dawson, to name several—were equally notable.

Olson had come to Black Mountain following publication of a most singular critical work on Melville, *Call Me Ishmael* (1947), which he had written with the help of a Guggenheim Fellowship.[1] In that book he makes clear his relation to a responsiveness and decision in such writing to be found only in such comparable works as D. H. Lawrence's *Studies in Classic American Literature*, W. C. Williams' *In The American Grain*, and Edward Dahlberg's *Can These Bones Live*. In this respect, criticism is not only a system of notation and categorization—it is an active and definitive engagement with what a text proposes. It is not merely a descriptive process. *Call Me Ishmael* begins:

> I take SPACE to be the central fact to man born in America, from Folsom cave to now. I spell it large because it comes large here. Large, and without mercy.
> It is geography at bottom, a hell of wide land from the beginning. That made the first American story (Parkman's): exploration . . .

Olson had also been in touch with Ezra Pound, who had recently been returned to the States to face trial on the charge of treason. There is a very moving defense of Pound written by Olson for the *Partisan Review*,[2] for whom he acted as a "reporter" in order to gain admittance to Pound's first arraignment in Washington. It is called "This Is Yeats Speaking"—the title itself a clear measure of those circumstances Pound's accusers were preparing to ignore. As Yeats, he says:

> We were the forerunners—Pound only the more extreme— but our time was out of phase and made us enders. Lawrence

---

[1] Shortly after, Olson received a second Fellowship, for a prose book, a collection of narratives, but it was never completed. One story, however, "Stocking Cap," appeared in the *Montevallo Review*, Vol. I, #2, Summer 1951.
[2] Vol. XIII, No. 1—Winter 1946.

among us alone had the true mask, he lacked the critical intelligence, and was prospective. You are the antithetical men,
and your time is forward, the conflict is more declared, it is for
you to hold the mirror up to authority, behind our respect for
which lay a disrespect for democracy as we were acquainted
with it. A slogan will not suffice . . .

2

Olson's approach was thus twice removed from the terms of
any other critical intelligence of that period. He spoke of
"geography" and that was clearly anti-literary. He proposed a
sense of the literal nature of this country quite distinct from
those critics influenced by European traditions. If he was involved with particular European evidences (as witness his trans-
lation of Rimbaud's last recorded poem, "Ô saisons, ô châteaux
. . . ," in "Variations Done for Gerald van de Weile"), he so
involved them that they became the American context equally:

> I offer, in explanation, a quote:
> si j'ai du goût, ce n'est guères
> que pour la terre et les pierres . . .
> ("The Kingfishers")

If I have any taste, it is only for earth and stones . . . Or to continue with Rimbaud's text from which this is also taken:

> Je déjeûne toujours d'air
> De roc, de charbons, de fer.[3]
>
> *Daily I dine on air,*
> *rock, coal, iron* . . .

It is relevant, then, that Olson's particular nature should lead
him in Yucatan[4] to just such exploration as he values in Parkman, or equally in Herodotus ("I would be an historian as
Herodotus was, looking / for oneself for the evidence of / what

---

[3] "Faim," *Delires II.*
[4] Olson lived in Lerma from December 1950 to July 1951. "Mayan
Letters" is a selection made from letters written to me at that time. In
1952 he was awarded a Wenner-Gren Foundation grant for further study
of Mayan hieroglyphs.

is said . . . ," "Letter 23," *The Maximus Poems*). In "Mayan Letters" we have unequivocal evidence of a *kind* of intelligence which cannot propose the assumption of content prior to its experience of that content, which *looks*, out of its *own* eyes. This does not mean that conjecture is to be absent, insofar as *jacio* means "throw" and *con*, "together"—however simply this point may note the actual process. It is a consistent fact with Olson that he does use his legs, and does depend on what his own instincts and intelligence can discover for him. In this way he *throws together* all he has come to possess.

But humanism, as a system of thought or ordering of persons in their relations to other things in the world, is distinctly absent. Even the most sympathetic ordering of human effects and intelligence leads to unavoidable assumptions, and the test— which is the reality of one's quite literal being—denies any investment of reality prior to its fact.

> There are no hierarchies, no infinite, no such
>   many as mass, there are only
> eyes in all heads,
> to be looked out of
>
>   ("Letter 6")

This commitment is further proposed and defined in "Human Universe," written, significantly, during that same period in Yucatan. We are not here involved with existentialism, despite the apparent closeness of sympathies at times. That is, Camus may speak of a world *without appeal*, but the system of discourse he makes use of is still demonstrably a closed one. What he seems most despairing about is that language cannot make sense of the world, that logic and classification do not lead to conclusions and value—but open only to the dilemma of experience itself. But *L'Étranger* is again a closed demonstration, a "fiction" proposed as example, and this, of course, is to stay within that universe of discourse which Olson distrusts.

> . . . such an analysis only accomplishes a *description*, does not
> come to grips with what really matters: that a thing, any thing,
> impinges on us by a more important fact, its self-existence, with-

out reference to any other thing, in short, the very character of it which calls our attention to it, which wants us to know more about it, its particularity. This is what we are confronted by, not the thing's "class," any hierarchy, of quality or quantity, but the thing itself, and its *relevance* to ourselves who are the experience of it (whatever it may mean to someone else, or whatever other relations it may have).

("Human Universe")

Camus despairs of his inability to fit experience to possible orders of language, whereas Olson would insist that language be returned to its place *in* experience, neither more nor less than any other act.

3

William Carlos Williams had said, "No ideas but in things," thereby insisting that reality was a real matter. Pound equally insisted, "Any tendency to abstract general statement is a greased slide." Both men have clearly to do with possibilities in writing of which Olson is the further evidence, but his own qualifications of either man are also relevant. For example, Pound he felt limited to an "ego-system":

> Ez's epic solves problems by his ego: his single emotion breaks all down to his equals or inferiors. . . . Which assumption, that there are intelligent men whom he can outtalk, is beautiful because it destroys historical time, and
> thus creates the methodology of the Cantos, viz, a space-field where, by inversion, though the material is all time material, he has driven through it so sharply by the beak of his ego, that, he has turned time into what we must now have, space & its live air. . . .

("Mayan Letters")

The gain is that any instance of intelligence is relevant insofar as it proves so, that what was said in 500 B.C. can be actively heard in 1965—and in that sense "time" is denied as a limit of such a possibility. But the dilemma it leads to is that the ego or mind is made the sole measure of such experience.

By contrast, Olson feels that Williams offers an *emotional*

5

system, which does not limit the context of writing to an assumption of *understanding*—or, better, it attains a way of writing that *feels* as it goes as well as *sees*. This allows the experience of writing to be more sensitive than the ego alone can admit.

In the second part of "Projective Verse,"[5] Olson makes this useful summary:

> Objectism is the getting rid of the lyrical interference of the individual as ego, of the "subject" and his soul, that peculiar presumption by which western man has interposed himself between what he is as a creature of nature (with certain instructions to carry out) and those other creations of nature which we may, with no derogation, call objects. For a man is himself an object, whatever he may take to be his advantages, the more likely to recognize himself as such the greater his advantages, particularly at that moment that he achieves an humilitas sufficient to make him of use.

4

When Williams first read "Projective Verse," his response was immediate:

> I share your excitement, it is as if the whole area lifted. It's the sort of thing we are after and must have . . . Everything in it leans on action, on the verb: one thing *leads* to another which is thereby activated . . .[6]

It was an excitement which many of us shared, because what confronted us in 1950 was a closed system indeed, poems patterned upon exterior and traditionally accepted models. The New Criticism of that period was dominant and would not admit the possibility of verse considered as an "open field."

But, thinking now of what else was clearly happening, that

[5] "Projective Verse" was first published in *Poetry New York*, Number Three, 1950. The date is significant.

[6] I take this from a letter Williams wrote me at the time. His interest is further demonstrated by the fact that he includes a substantial section of Olson's "Projective Verse" in his *Autobiography*.

attitude was already losing ground. If one reads Jackson Pollock's comments on his painting at that time, he can note for himself the obvious parallel:

> When I am *in* my painting, I'm not aware of what I'm doing. It is only after a sort of "get acquainted" period that I see what I have been about. I have no fears about making changes, destroying the image, etc., because the painting has a life of its own. I try to let it come through. It is only when I lose contact with the painting that the result is a mess. Otherwise there is pure harmony, an easy give and take, and the painting comes out well.[7]

A like situation was clear in the work of John Cage, which involved the introduction of "chance" factors and reconsidered the whole context of a "melodic" modality in music. And similar circumstances were very clear in the sciences as well. "Formal" order, taken as a *sine qua non*, could no longer be assumed as a necessary virtue.

How, then, manage its alternatives—in such a way that the result be not random but rather the most precise discrimination and attention of which the man writing is capable? Olson's premise is this:

> A poem is energy transferred from where the poet got it (he will have some several causations), by way of the poem itself to, all the way over to, the reader . . .
>
> ("Projective Verse")

This means, very literally, that a poem is some *thing*, a structure possessed of its own organization in turn derived from the circumstances of its making. Thus far, it could, of course, be a sonnet—and under given circumstances well might be, supposing that the man writing discovered that possibility as he did, in fact, write. But what one is saying has intimate relation to how one is saying it—and/or the content, in this sense, is that which qualifies the possibilities of form. Valéry, in *The Art of Poetry*, qualifies as *lyric* that mode of poetry in which the content and the form are realized simultaneously. Neither one can precede

---

[7] "Problems of Contemporary Art," *Possibilities 1*, 1947-8.

the other as a possibility. It is this sense, then, which Olson extends to all occasions of writing in verse. It is hardly a careless procedure, in that no order more than that so recognized can be gained. Apropos the syllable, "the king and pin of versification," Olson writes:

> It is by their syllables that words juxtapose in beauty, by these particles of sound as clearly as by the sense of the words which they compose. In any given instance, because there is a choice of words, the choice, if a man is in there, will be, spontaneously, the obedience of his ear to the syllables . . .
>
> ("Projective Verse")

The capabilities of that ear will have no other evidence to support them but that which they define. "Prosody," Pound said, "is the articulation of the total sound of a poem." In the note to which this serves as motto, so to speak, Olson says:

> It's as though you were hearing for the first time—who knows what a poem ought to sound like? until it's thar? And how do you get it thar except as you do—*you*, and nobody else (who's a poet
> What's
> a poem?
> It ain't dreamt until it walks   It talks   It spreads its green barrazza
> Listen closely, folks, this poem comes to you by benefit of its own Irish green bazoo. You take it, from here.
>
> ("A Foot Is to Kick With,"
> *Human Universe and Other Essays*)

5

The range of materials here collected is not evidence of "subjects" or of some preoccupation with any such term of argument. "Letter 15" notes that clearly enough: "He sd, 'You go all around the subject.' And I sd, 'I didn't know it was a subject . . .' " It is worth some thought.

Where one lives is a complex occasion, both inside and out. What we have as *place* is defined in "The Resistance," and, again, it is not only "existential." When a man walks down a street, he walks it only *now*—whether the date be 1860, 1960, or so-called centuries ago. History is a literal story, the activity of evidence.

In short, the world is not separable, and we *are* in it. The fact of "Apollonius of Tyana" is not *then,* so to speak—at some remove in time because its person is, as we might say, historical. Each moment is evidence of its own content, and all that is met with in it, is as present as anything else. Apollonius *is* a present instance.

The most insistent concern I find in Olson's writing is the intent to gain the particular experience of any possibility in life, so that no abstraction intervenes. "In Cold Hell, In Thicket" makes clear the difficulties, and "To Gerhardt, There, Among Europe's Things," the situation of the specifically American:

> . . . Or come here
> where we will welcome you
> with nothing but what is . . .

A dream *is*—as clearly as whatever else. The circumstance of "The Librarian" or "As the Dead Prey Upon Us" will not be confusing to any who admit what they *know* to be a total content, rather than one divided by assumptions of understanding. "In dreams begin responsibilites . . ." I was moved on hearing Williams use that quotation from Yeats at the outset of his acceptance speech for the National Book Award in the early fifties. But it is not only "responsibilities," but also "This very thing you are . . ."

Meaning is not importantly *referential*. Reference may well prove *relevant*—but I can make myself clearer by quoting a sense of *meaning* which Olson used at the Berkeley Poetry Conference this past summer (1965): *That which exists through itself is what is called the meaning.* He also noted, as a usable context for that "mapping" or measure of how one is where one is, these four terms:

> *earth*
> *Imago Mundi*
> *history*
> *Anima Mundi*

9

By "earth" is meant all that literal ground we walk on and its specific character, including water and sky; by "Imago Mundi," that way of seeing or view of existence evident in any particular circumstance of life; by "history," all the condition and accumulation of human acts and effects, as these exist; by "Anima Mundi," that which informs and quickens life in its own condition, the spirit—or what we speak of in saying, "the *quick* and the dead." I offer these simply as measure, for the relevance of what follows.

Placitas, New Mexico   ROBERT CREELEY
October 3, 1965

I

THE RESISTANCE

for Jean Riboud

This is eternity. This now. This foreshortened span.

Men will recognize it more easily (& dwell in it so) when we regain what the species lost, how long ago: nature's original intention with the organism, that it live 130 years. Or so Bogomolets' researches into the nature of connective tissue seem to prove. True or not, with or without aid from his own biosis, man has no alternative: his mortal years are his enemy. He accepts this new position. It is the root act.

There are other aids. Time, for example, has been cut down to size, though I do not think that those who have come to the knowledge of now came here from that powerful abstraction space-time, no matter how its corrections of time reinforce the position.

Man came here by an intolerable way. When man is reduced to so much fat for soap, superphosphate for soil, fillings and shoes for sale, he has, to begin again, one answer, one point of resistance only to such fragmentation, one organized ground, a ground he comes to by a way the precise contrary of the cross, of spirit in the old sense, in old mouths. It is his own physiology he is forced to arrive at. And the way—the way of the beast, of man and the Beast.

It is his body that is his answer, his body intact and fought for, the absolute of his organism in its simplest terms, this structure evolved by nature, repeated in each act of birth, the animal man; the house he is, this house that moves, breathes, acts, this house where his life is, where he dwells against the enemy, against the beast.

Or the fraud. This organism now our citadel never was cathedral, draughty tenement of soul, was what it is: ground, stone, wall, cannon, tower. In this intricate structure are we based, now more certainly than ever (besieged, overthrown), for its power is bone muscle nerve blood brain   a man, its fragile mortal force its old eternity, resistance.

PROJECTIVE   VERSE

(projectile   (percussive   (prospective

vs.

The NON-Projective

(*or what a French critic calls "closed" verse, that verse which print bred and which is pretty much what we have had, in English & American, and have still got, despite the work of Pound & Williams:*

it led Keats, already a hundred years ago, to see it (Wordsworth's, Milton's) in the light of "the Egotistical Sublime"; and it persists, at this latter day, as what you might call the private-soul-at-any-public-wall)

Verse now, 1950, if it is to go ahead, if it is to be of *essential* use, must, I take it, catch up and put into itself certain laws and possibilities of the breath, of the breathing of the man who writes as well as of his listenings. (The revolution of the ear, 1910, the trochee's heave, asks it of the younger poets.)

I want to do two things: first, try to show what projective or OPEN verse is, what it involves, in its act of composition, how, in distinction from the non-projective, it is accomplished; and II, suggest a few ideas about what stance toward reality brings such verse into being, what that stance does, both to the poet and to his reader. (The stance involves, for example, a change beyond, and larger than, the technical, and may, the way things look, lead to new poetics and to new concepts from which some sort of drama, say, or of epic, perhaps, may emerge.)

15

First, some simplicities that a man learns, if he works in OPEN, or what can also be called COMPOSITION BY FIELD, as opposed to inherited line, stanza, over-all form, what is the "old" base of the non-projective.

(1) the *kinetics* of the thing. A poem is energy transferred from where the poet got it (he will have some several causations), by way of the poem itself to, all the way over to, the reader. Okay. Then the poem itself must, at all points, be a high energy-construct and, at all points, an energy-discharge. So: how is the poet to accomplish same energy, how is he, what is the process by which a poet gets in, at all points energy at least the equivalent of the energy which propelled him in the first place, yet an energy which is peculiar to verse alone and which will be, obviously, also different from the energy which the reader, because he is a third term, will take away?

This is the problem which any poet who departs from closed form is specially confronted by. And it involves a whole series of new recognitions. From the moment he ventures into FIELD COMPOSITION—put himself in the open—he can go by no track other than the one the poem under hand declares, for itself. Thus he has to behave, and be, instant by instant, aware of some several forces just now beginning to be examined. (It is much more, for example, this push, than simply such a one as Pound put, so wisely, to get us started: "the musical phrase," go by it, boys, rather than by, the metronome.)

(2) is the *principle*, the law which presides conspicuously over such composition, and, when obeyed, is the reason why a projective poem can come into being. It is this: FORM IS NEVER MORE THAN AN EXTENSION OF CONTENT. (Or so it got phrased by one, R. Creeley, and it makes absolute sense to me, with this possible corollary, that right form, in any given poem, is the only and exclusively possible extension of content under hand.) There it is, brothers, sitting there, for USE.

Now (3) the *process* of the thing, how the principle can be made so to shape the energies that the form is accomplished. And I think it can be boiled down to one statement (first pounded into my head by Edward Dahlberg): ONE PERCEPTION MUST IMMEDIATELY AND DIRECTLY LEAD TO A FURTHER PERCEPTION. It means exactly what it says, is a matter of, at *all* points (even, I should say, of our management of daily reality as of the daily work) get on with it, keep moving, keep in, speed, the nerves, their speed, the perceptions, theirs, the acts, the split second acts, the whole business, keep it moving as fast as you can, citizen. And if you also set up as a poet, USE USE USE the process at all points, in any given poem always, always one perception must must must MOVE, INSTANTER, ON ANOTHER!

So there we are, fast, there's the dogma. And its excuse, its usableness, in practice. Which gets us, it ought to get us, inside the machinery, now, 1950, of how projective verse is made.

If I hammer, if I recall in, and keep calling in, the breath, the breathing as distinguished from the hearing, it is for cause, it is to insist upon a part that breath plays in verse which has not (due, I think, to the smothering of the power of the line by too set a concept of foot) has not been sufficiently observed or practiced, but which has to be if verse is to advance to its proper force and place in the day, now, and ahead. I take it that PROJECTIVE VERSE teaches, is, this lesson, that that verse will only do in which a poet manages to register both the acquisitions of his ear *and* the pressures of his breath.

Let's start from the smallest particle of all, the syllable. It is the king and pin of versification, what rules and holds together the lines, the larger forms, of a poem. I would suggest that verse here and in England dropped this secret from the late Elizabethans to Ezra Pound, lost it, in the sweetness of meter and rime, in a honey-head. (The syllable is one way to distinguish the original success of blank verse, and its falling off, with Milton.)

It is by their syllables that words juxtapose in beauty, by these particles of sound as clearly as by the sense of the words

17

which they compose. In any given instance, because there is a choice of words, the choice, if a man is in there, will be, spontaneously, the obedience of his ear to the syllables. The fineness, and the practice, lie here, at the minimum and source of speech.

> O western wynd, when wilt thou blow
> And the small rain down shall rain
> O Christ that my love were in my arms
> And I in my bed again

It would do no harm, as an act of correction to both prose and verse as now written, if both rime and meter, and, in the quantity words, both sense and sound, were less in the forefront of the mind than the syllable, if the syllable, that fine creature, were more allowed to lead the harmony on. With this warning, to those who would try: to step back here to this place of the elements and minims of language, is to engage speech where it is least careless—and least logical. Listening for the syllables must be so constant and so scrupulous, the exaction must be so complete, that the assurance of the ear is purchased at the highest—40 hours a day—price. For from the root out, from all over the place, the syllable comes, the figures of, the dance:

"Is" comes from the Aryan root, *as*, to breathe. The English "not" equals the Sanscrit *na*, which may come from the root *na*, to be lost, to perish. "Be" is from *bhu*, to grow.

I say the syllable, king, and that it is spontaneous, this way: the ear, the ear which has collected, which has listened, the ear, which is so close to the mind that it is the mind's, that it has the mind's speed . . .

it is close, another way: the mind is brother to this sister and is, because it is so close, is the drying force, the incest, the sharpener . . .

it is from the union of the mind and the ear that the syllable is born.

But the syllable is only the first child of the incest of verse (always, that Egyptian thing, it produces twins!). The other child is the LINE. And together, these two, the syllable *and* the line, they make a poem, they make that thing, the—what shall we call it, the Boss of all, the "Single Intelligence." And the line comes (I swear it) from the breath, from the breathing of the man who writes, at the moment that he writes, and thus is, it is here that, the daily work, the WORK, gets in, for only he, the man who writes, can declare, at every moment, the line its metric and its ending—where its breathing, shall come to, termination.

The trouble with most work, to my taking, since the breaking away from traditional lines and stanzas, and from such wholes as, say, Chaucer's *Troilus* or S's *Lear*, is: contemporary workers go lazy RIGHT HERE WHERE THE LINE IS BORN.

Let me put it baldly. The two halves are:
the HEAD, by way of the EAR, to the SYLLABLE
the HEART, by way of the BREATH, to the LINE
And the joker? that it is in the 1st half of the proposition that, in composing, one lets-it-rip; and that it is in the 2nd half, surprise, it is the LINE that's the baby that gets, as the poem is getting made, the attention, the control, that it is right here, in the line, that the shaping takes place, each moment of the going.

I am dogmatic, that the head shows in the syllable. The dance of the intellect is there, among them, prose or verse. Consider the best minds you know in this here business: where does the head show, is it not, precise, here, in the swift currents of the syllable? can't you tell a brain when you see what it does, just there? It is true, what the master says he picked up from Confusion: all the thots men are capable of can be entered on the back of a postage stamp. So, is it not the PLAY of a mind we are after, is not that that shows whether a mind is there at all?

And the threshing floor for the dance? Is it anything but the LINE? And when the line has, is, a deadness, is it not a heart which has gone lazy, is it not, suddenly, slow things, similes, say, adjectives, or such, that we are bored by?

For there is a whole flock of rhetorical devices which have now to be brought under a new bead, now that we sight with the line. Simile is only one bird who comes down, too easily. The descriptive functions generally have to be watched, every second, in projective verse, because of their easiness, and thus their drain on the energy which composition by field allows into a poem. Any slackness takes off attention, that crucial thing, from the job in hand, from the *push* of the line under hand at the moment, under the reader's eye, in his moment. Observation of any kind is, like argument in prose, properly previous to the act of the poem, and, if allowed in, must be so juxtaposed, apposed, set in, that it does not, for an instant, sap the going energy of the content toward its form.

It comes to this, this whole aspect of the newer problems. (We now enter, actually, the large area of the whole poem, into the FIELD, if you like, where all the syllables and all the lines must be managed in their relations to each other.) It is a matter, finally, of OBJECTS, what they are, what they are inside a poem, how they got there, and, once there, how they are to be used. This is something I want to get to in another way in Part II, but, for the moment, let me indicate this, that every element in an open poem (the syllable, the line, as well as the image, the sound, the sense) must be taken up as participants in the kinetic of the poem just as solidly as we are accustomed to take what we call the objects of reality; and that these elements are to be seen as creating the tensions of a poem just as totally as do those other objects create what we know as the world.

The objects which occur at every given moment of composition (of recognition, we can call it) are, can be, must be treated exactly as they do occur therein and not by any ideas or preconceptions from outside the poem, must be handled as a series of objects in field in such a way that a series of tensions (which they also are) are made to *hold*, and to hold exactly inside the content and the context of the poem which has forced itself, through the poet and them, into being.

Because breath allows *all* the speech-force of language back in (speech is the "solid" of verse, is the secret of a poem's energy), because, now, a poem has, by speech, solidity, everything in it can now be treated as solids, objects, things; and, though insisting upon the absolute difference of the reality of verse from that other dispersed and distributed thing, yet each of these elements of a poem can be allowed to have the play of their separate energies and can be allowed, once the poem is well composed, to keep, as those other objects do, their proper confusions.

Which brings us up, immediately, bang, against tenses, in fact against syntax, in fact against grammar generally, that is, as we have inherited it. Do not tenses, must they not also be kicked around anew, in order that time, that other governing absolute, may be kept, as must the space-tensions of a poem, immediate, contemporary to the acting-on-you of the poem? I would argue that here, too, the LAW OF THE LINE, which projective verse creates, must be hewn to, obeyed, and that the conventions which logic has forced on syntax must be broken open as quietly as must the too set feet of the old line. But an analysis of how far a new poet can stretch the very conventions on which communication by language rests, is too big for these notes, which are meant, I hope it is obvious, merely to get things started.

Let me just throw in this. It is my impression that *all* parts of speech suddenly, in composition by field, are fresh for both sound and percussive use, spring up like unknown, unnamed vegetables in the patch, when you work it, come spring. Now take Hart Crane. What strikes me in him is the singleness of the push to the nominative, his push along that one arc of freshness, the attempt to get back to word as handle. (If logos is word as thought, what is word as noun, as, pass me that, as Newman Shea used to ask, at the galley table, put a jib on the blood, will ya.) But there is a loss in Crane of what Fenollosa is so right about, in syntax, the sentence as first act of nature, as lightning, as passage of force from subject to object, quick, in this case, from Hart to me, in every case, from me to you, the VERB, between two nouns. Does not Hart miss the advantages, by such an isolated push, miss the point of the whole front of syllable, line, field, and what happened to all language, and to the poem, as a result?

I return you now to London, to beginnings, to the syllable, for the pleasures of it, to intermit:

> If music be the food of love, play on,
> give me excess of it, that, surfeiting,
> the appetite may sicken, and so die.
> That strain again. It had a dying fall,
> o, it came over my ear like the sweet sound
> that breathes upon a bank of violets,
> stealing and giving odour.

What we have suffered from, is manuscript, press, the removal of verse from its producer and its reproducer, the voice, a removal by one, by two removes from its place of origin *and* its destination. For the breath has a double meaning which latin had not yet lost.

The irony is, from the machine has come one gain not yet sufficiently observed or used, but which leads directly on toward projective verse and its consequences. It is the advantage of the typewriter that, due to its rigidity and its space precisions, it can, for a poet, indicate exactly the breath, the pauses, the suspensions even of syllables, the juxtapositions even of parts of phrases, which he intends. For the first time the poet has the stave and the bar a musician has had. For the first time he can, without the convention of rime and meter, record the listening he has done to his own speech and by that one act indicate how he would want any reader, silently or otherwise, to voice his work.

It is time we picked the fruits of the experiments of Cummings, Pound, Williams, each of whom has, after his way, already used the machine as a scoring to his composing, as a script to its vocalization. It is now only a matter of the recognition of the conventions of composition by field for us to bring into being an open verse as formal as the closed, with all its traditional advantages.

If a contemporary poet leaves a space as long as the phrase before it, he means that space to be held, by the breath, an equal length of time. If he suspends a word or syllable at the end of a line (this was most Cummings' addition) he means that time to pass that it takes the eye—that hair of time suspended—to pick up the next line. If he wishes a pause so light it hardly separates the words, yet does not want a comma—which is an interruption of the meaning rather than the sounding of the line—follow him when he uses a symbol the typewriter has ready to hand:

"What does not change / is the will to change"

Observe him, when he takes advantage of the machine's multiple margins, to juxtapose:

"Sd he:
    to dream takes no effort
    to think is easy
        to act is more difficult

    but for a man to act after he has taken thought, this!
is the most difficult thing of all"

Each of these lines is a progressing of both the meaning and the breathing forward, and then a backing up, without a progress or any kind of movement outside the unit of time local to the idea.

There is more to be said in order that this convention be recognized, especially in order that the revolution out of which it came may be so forwarded that work will get published to offset the reaction now afoot to return verse to inherited forms of cadence and rime. But what I want to emphasize here, by this emphasis on the typewriter as the personal and instantaneous recorder of the poet's work, is the already projective nature of verse as the sons of Pound and Williams are practicing it. Already they are composing as though verse was to have the reading its writing involved, as though not the eye but the ear was to be its measurer, as though the intervals of its composition could be so carefully put down as to be precisely the intervals of its registration. For the ear, which once had the burden of memory to quicken it (rime & regular cadence were its aids and have merely lived on in print after the oral necessities were ended) can now again, that the poet has his means, be the threshold of projective verse.

II

Which gets us to what I promised, the degree to which the projective involves a stance toward reality outside a poem as well as a new stance towards the reality of a poem itself. It is a matter of content, the content of Homer or of Euripides or of Seami as distinct from that which I might call the more "literary" masters. From the moment the projective purpose of the act of verse is recognized, the content does—it will—change. If the beginning and the end is breath, voice in its largest sense, then the material of verse shifts. It has to. It starts with the composer. The dimension of his line itself changes, not to speak of the change in his conceiving, of the matter he will turn to, of the scale in which he imagines that matter's use. I myself would pose the difference by a physical image. It is no accident that Pound and Williams both were involved variously in a movement which got called "objectivism." But that word was then used in some sort of a necessary quarrel, I take it, with "subjectivism." It is now too late to be bothered with the latter. It has excellently done itself to death, even though we are all caught in its dying. What seems to me a more valid formulation for present use is "objectism," a word to be taken to stand for the kind of relation of man to experience which a poet might state as the necessity of a line or a work to be as wood is, to be as clean as wood is as it issues from the hand of nature, to be shaped as wood can be when a man has had his hand to it. Objectism is the getting rid of the lyrical interference of the individual as ego, of the "subject" and his soul, that peculiar presumption by which western man has interposed himself between what he is as a creature of nature (with certain instructions to carry out) and those other creations of nature which we may, with no derogation, call objects. For a man is himself an object, whatever he may take to be his advantages, the more likely to recognize himself as such the greater his advantages, particularly at that moment that he achieves an humilitas sufficient to make him of use.

It comes to this: the use of a man, by himself and thus by others, lies in how he conceives his relation to nature, that force to which he owes his somewhat small existence. If he sprawl, he shall find little to sing but himself, and shall sing, nature has such paradoxical ways, by way of artificial forms outside himself. But if he stays inside himself, if he is contained within his nature as he is participant in the larger force, he will be able to listen, and his hearing through himself will give him secrets objects share. And by an inverse law his shapes will make their own way. It is in this sense that the projective act, which is the artist's act in the larger field of objects, leads to dimensions larger than the man. For a man's problem, the moment he takes speech up in all its fullness, is to give his work his seriousness, a seriousness sufficient to cause the thing he makes to try to take its place alongside the things of nature. This is not easy. Nature works from reverence, even in her destructions (species go down with a crash). But breath is man's special qualification as animal. Sound is a dimension he has extended. Language is one of his proudest acts. And when a poet rests in these as they are in himself (in his physiology, if you like, but the life in him, for all that) then he, if he chooses to speak from these roots, works in that area where nature has given him size, projective size.

It is projective size that the play, *The Trojan Women*, possesses, for it is able to stand, is it not, as its people do, beside the Aegean—and neither Andromache or the sea suffer diminution. In a less "heroic" but equally "natural" dimension Seami causes the Fisherman and the Angel to stand clear in *Hagoromo*. And Homer, who is such an unexamined cliche that I do not think I need to press home in what scale Nausicaa's girls wash their clothes.

Such works, I should argue—and I use them simply because their equivalents are yet to be done—could not issue from men who conceived verse without the full relevance of human voice, without reference to where lines come from, in the individual who writes. Nor do I think it accident that, at this end point of the argument, I should use, for examples, two dramatists and an epic poet. For I would hazard the guess that, if projective verse is practiced long enough, is driven ahead hard enough along the course I think it dictates, verse again can carry much larger material than it has carried in our language since the Elizabethans. But it can't be jumped. We are only at its beginnings, and if I think that the *Cantos* make more "dramatic" sense than do the plays of Mr. Eliot, it is not because I think they have solved the problem but because the methodology of the verse in them points a way by which, one day, the problem of larger content and of larger forms may be solved. Eliot is, in fact, a proof of a present danger, of "too easy" a going on the practice of verse as it has been, rather than as it must be, practiced. There is no question, for example, that Eliot's line, from "Prufrock" on down, has speech-force, is "dramatic," is, in fact, one of the most notable lines since Dryden. I suppose it stemmed immediately to him from Browning, as did so many of Pound's early things. In any case Eliot's line has obvious relations backward to the Elizabethans, especially to the soliloquy. Yet O. M. Eliot is *not* projective. It could even be argued (and I say this carefully, as I have said all things about the non-projective, having considered how each of us must save himself after his own fashion and how much, for that matter, each of us owes to the non-projective, and will continue to owe, as both go alongside each other) but it could be argued that it is because Eliot has stayed inside the non-projective that he fails as a dramatist—that his root is the mind alone, and a scholastic mind at that (no high *intelletto* despite his apparent clarities)—and that, in his listenings he has stayed there where the ear and the mind are, has only gone from his fine ear outward rather than, as I say a projective poet will, down through the workings of his own throat to that place where breath comes from, where breath has its beginnings, where drama has to come from, where, the coincidence is, all act springs.

Poetry New York No. 3, 1950

LETTER TO ELAINE FEINSTEIN

May, 1959

DEAR E. B. FEINSTEIN,

Your questions catch me athwart any new sense I might have of a "poetics." The best previous throw I made on it was in *Poetry NY* some years ago on Projective Open or Field verse versus Closed, with much on the *line* and the *syllable.*

The basic idea anyway for me is that one, that form is never any more than an extension of content—a non-literary sense, certainly. I believe in Truth! (Wahrheit) My sense is that beauty (Schönheit) better stay in the thingitself: das Ding— Ja!—macht ring (the attack, I suppose, on the "completed thought," or, the Idea, yes? Thus the syntax question: what is the sentence?)

The only advantage of speech rhythms (to take your 2nd question 1st) is illiteracy: the non-literary, exactly in Dante's sense of the value of the vernacular over grammar—that speech as a communicator is prior to the individual and is picked up as soon as and with ma's milk . . . he said nurse's tit. In other words, speech rhythm only as anyone of us has it, if we come on from the line of force as piped in as well as from piping we very much have done up to this moment—if we have, from, that "common" not grammatical source. The "source" question is damned interesting today—as Shelley saw, like Dante, that, if it comes in, that way, primary, from Ma there is then a double line of chromosomic giving (A) the inherent speech (thought, power) the "species," that is; and (B) the etymological: this is where I find "foreign" languages so wild, especially the Indo-European line with the advantage now that we have Hittite to back up to. I couldn't stress enough on this speech rhythm question the pay-off in *traction* that a non-literate, non-commercial and non-historical constant daily experience of tracking *any* word, practically, one finds oneself using, back along its line of force to Anglo-Saxon, Latin, Greek, and out to Sanskrit, or now, if someone wld do it, some "dictionary" of roots which wld include Hittite at least.

I'll give in a minute the connection of this to form if capturable in the poem, that is, the usual "poetics" biz, but excuse me if I hammer shortly the immense help archaeology, and some specific linguistic scholarship—actually, from my experience mainly of such completely different "grammars" as North American Indians present, in the present syntax hangup: like Hopi. But also Trobriand space-Time premises. And a couple of North California tongues, like Yani. But it is the archaeology *behind* our own history proper, Hittite, for the above reason, but now that Canaanite is known (Ugaritic) and Sumerian, and the direct connection of the Celts to the Aryans and so to the Achaean-Trojan forbears which has *slowed* and opened the speech language thing as we got it, now, in our hands, to make it do more form than how form got set by Sappho & Homer, and hasn't changed much since.

I am talking from a new "double axis": the replacement of the Classical-representational by the *primitive-abstract* ((if this all sounds bloody German, excuse the weather, it's from the east today, and wet)). I mean of course not at all primitive in that stupid use of it as opposed to civilized. One means it now as "primary," as how one finds anything, pick it up as one does new—fresh/first. Thus one is equal across history forward and back, and it's all levy, as present is, but sd that way, one states . . . a different space-time. Content, in other words, is also shifted—at least from humanism, as we've had it since the Indo-Europeans got their fid in there (circum 1500 B.C.) ((Note: I'm for 'em on the muse level, and agin 'em on the content, or "Psyche" side.

Which gets me to yr 1st question—"the use of the Image." "the Image" (wow, that you capitalize it makes *sense*: it is *all* we had (post-circum *The Two Noble Kinsmen*), as we had a sterile grammar (an insufficient "sentence") we had analogy only: images, no matter how learned or how simple: even Burns say, allowing etc and including Frost! Comparison. Thus representation was never off the dead-spot of description. Nothing was *happening* as of the poem itself—ding and zing or something. It was referential to reality. And that a p. poor crawling actuarial "real"—good enough to keep banks and insurance companies, plus mediocre governments etc. But not Poetry's *Truth* like my friends from the American Underground cry and spit in the face of "Time."

The Image also has to be taken by a double: that is, if you bisect a parabola you get an enantiomorph (The Hopi say what goes on over there isn't happening here therefore it isn't the same: pure "localism" of space-time, but such localism can now be called: what you find out for yrself (*'istorin*) keeps all accompanying circumstance.

The basic trio wld seem to be: topos/typos/tropos, 3 in 1. The "blow" hits here, and me, "bent" as born and of sd one's own decisions for better or worse (allowing clearly, by Jesus Christ, that you do love or go down)

if this sounds "mystical" I plead so. Wahrheit: I find the contemporary substitution of society for the cosmos captive and deathly.

Image, therefore, is vector. It carries the trinity via the double to the single form which one makes oneself able, if so, to issue from the "content" (multiplicity: originally, and repetitively, chaos—Tiamat: wot the Hindo-Europeans knocked out by giving the Old Man (Juice himself) all the lightning.

The Double, then, (the "home"/heartland/of the post-Mesopotamians AND the post-Hindo Eees:

At the moment it comes out   the Muse ("world"
                             ———————————————————
                             the Psyche (the "life"

You wld know already I'm buggy on say the Proper Noun, so much so I wld take it Pun is Rime, all from tope/type/trope, that built in is the connection, in each of us, to Cosmos, and if one taps, via psyche, plus a "true" adherence of Muse, one does reveal "Form"

in other words the "right" (wahr-) proper noun, however apparently idiosyncratic, if "tested" by one's own experience (out plus in) ought to yield along this phylo-line (as the speech thing, above) because—*decently* what one oneself can know, as well as what the word *means*—ontogenetic.

The other part is certainly "landscape"—the other part of the double of Image to "noun." By Landscape I mean what "narrative"; scene; event; climax; crisis; hero; development; posture; all that *meant*—all the substantive of what we call literary. To animate the scene today: wow: You say "orientate me." Yessir. Place it!

again

I drag it back: Place (topos, plus one's own bent plus what one *can* know, makes it possible to name.

O.K. I'm running out of appetite. Let this swirl—a bit like Crab Nebula—do for now. And please come back on me if you are interested. *Yrs.*

CHARLES OLSON

QUANTITY IN VERSE, AND SHAKESPEARE'S LATE PLAYS

(The argument: in the ten years from 1602 to the theatrical season 1612-13, from Campion's *Observations in the Art of English Poesie* through Shakespeare's last two plays HENRY 8 and THE TWO NOBLE KINSMEN, quantity made enough change in verse and Shakespeare enough change in comedy to take form all the way over

To chart it:

(I) in 1603-04 the first signs —TROILUS & CRESSIDA
MEASURE FOR MEASURE
(II) by 1607-08 change shows—TIMON OF ATHENS
and most in   PERICLES OF TYRE
(CORIOLANUS is written the same year and is
the final accentual blank verse tragedy.)

In the fall of 1609, Shakespeare's company moved indoors, into the Blackfriars theater, and in that first season the takings increased by £1000, or better than $50,000 in modern buying power.

(III) The Evidence, the season of 1610-11:

CYMBELINE (performed April, 1611)
THE WINTER'S TALE (performed
May 15, 1611)
THE TEMPEST (performed November 1)

In these plays the change of form is altogether clear, Tasso or Ariosto regained, MIDSUMMER NIGHT'S DREAM retaken, PLUS.

(IV) Verse-wise, for myself the full pleasure of quantity is most evident in Shakespeare's part with Fletcher in HENRY 8, and, above all, in THE TWO NOBLE KINSMEN, both done 1612-13

The late plays of Shakespeare are aerodynes, in which, by a series of baffles (the verse, with its emphasis on quantities), they have their power straight from the element they move in, that they displace, and they go in speed from zero to as fast as sound. They are motion, not action—by power of vacuum, they use it and occupy it at the same time. Though the plays exploit the earlier "Comedies," music, dance, spectacle, particularly *Midsummer Night's Dream* (it is turned back as the Italians are turned to), these earlier things only resemble the later as flying machines: they go in the air, that's all. The later plays move without internal combustion, or show any blades throwing the air. They come as quietly to a stop as they take off, vertically. They hover, they do whatever they are of a mind to do, one is not in the presence of drama or poem so known. These things (*Winter's Tale, Tempest, Two Noble Kinsmen*) are forms of power not known.

For two literary reasons: the fashioning of the verse, which takes the English language off where it was stuck, on its own motor power, on accent, on that "flow," those—"wings"; and the matter of the thought: these are comedies all right, but hardly Bottom or Beatrice (his Beatrice), neither the old rustic comic nor any light urban witty, nor magic faery spirit pleasant illusion of forest night streams, Nature that is. Shakespeare is no longer a Humanist in which Nature and Man are separate delights, or she is rank and he is his own wheel of fire. What these plays are is comedy in the sense another man was after who put it:

So Comedy is a certain kind of poetic narration differing from all others. It differs then from tragedy in its *content*, in that tragedy begins admirably and tranquilly, whereas its exit is foul and terrible, it is fetid, like a goat; but comedy introduces some *harsh* complication yet brings its matter to a *prosperous* end.

(Prospero's end.)

Throughout *De Vulgare Eloquentia* and *Epistola* X (from which the above is taken) Dante awards a more satisfying possibility to comedy than to tragedy, and for cause. As he puts it at the close of this letter to Can Grande della Scala:

> The end of the whole and the part may be manifold, to wit, the proximate *and* the ultimate. But dropping all subtle investigation, we may say briefly that the end of the whole and the part is *to remove those living in this life from the state of misery and lead them to the state of felicity.*

I would make no more of this than that Shakespeare, by and about 1610, age 46, wanted comedy to do that which Dante also made it do: enjoin. "As we are men," says Theseus at the end of the first scene of *The Two Noble Kinsmen*, "Thus should we do." I wish only to establish that these plays are different in that they are injunctive, so that they no longer need sit in the confusion of definition in which they have—romantical-tragical, tragical-comical, pastoral-wittical, whatever.

Beyond that, Shakespeare had no such frame as Christianity to set his vision of "felicity" in, as Dante had. He was a man of the Renaissance, and an Englishman, and what he took it could lead the living from misery stays secular. What Theseus says is

> Thus should we do. Being sensually subdued we lose our human title.

It is that title which Shakespeare is at pains to spell out the terms of, and by so doing to insure it, by 1610 and after.

What is more important and the most difference from Dante, as well as from Shakespeare's own previous art—and most since, for that matter—is that he makes form itself secular. I am imagining that form (one means simply the power a thing of art asserts by which it seizes, and both art and the observer are changed thereafter) has left its former places and though the means and the matter seem the same, it uses them so differently one is fooled if one looks for them as one used to, in the place where form was, in the sound of motors, brilliance in the sky. Form is now as much an invention as it always is. What is missed is, that it is. Verse and thoughts are vernacular. Who would have thought it! The absolute, in all its guises, even the smallest—notion opinion self-assertion—has slunk away. A huge difference has come about, something previously unknown about both the real and the natural has been disclosed: that the artificial (paradis n'est pas artificiel) the mechanical the arbitrary whatever you want to call the aesthetic, is not separate from them. It is what the felicity in these plays leads to, it does not lead to its own pursuit (this is the pathetic fallacy of humanism) it goes directly back to the real but in so doing a real and natural which are themselves transposed. It is my purpose to show that.

I

The limit on new in the verse is syntax. Shakespeare did not particularly disturb the working sentence as it had served him and others in blank verse proper. Imagery likewise. It is gone into as the sentence does, explicit, and descriptive. Yet the thought increases a verticality gained by blank verse itself between 1600 and 1608, and quantity (which tends at any time to increase the standing as against the running power of verse) most makes the language different. A pattern is seen: logicality persists in the syntax and image but the thinking and weighing in of the quantity stop twist and intensify the speech, thus increasing the instancy. In this situation it is the vocabulary which tips the scale, the increase (for good reasons of comedy and quantity, as we shall see) of the simplest monosyllables on the one hand, and, on the other, of the most intellective polysyllables. The result is a poetry with a perspective which blank verse, in its extensivity, could not supply.

One does not have to go outside *The Tempest* to show these things: the monosyllables at their quietest and sweetest,

> (Ceres, most bounteous lady, thy rich leas)
> of wheat, rye, barley, vetches, oats and peas;

consonants forced to the vertical,

> Thy banks with pioned and twilled brims
> which spongy April at thy hest betrims
> to make cold nymphs chaste crowns;

and the difference even when the basic sentence and image holds,

> Here thought they to have done
> some wanton charm upon this man and maid
> whose vows are that no bed-right shall be paid
> till Hymen's torch be lighted. But in vain.
> Mars' hot minion is returned again,
> her waspish-headed son has broke his arrows
> swears he will shoot no more but play with sparrows
> and be a boy right out.

But because *The Two Noble Kinsmen* is even left out of most canons as not Shakespeare's! and *Henry 8* is just let in, and both contain so much of just the order of power here asserted, I pick up on a speech from the latter play, Norfolk's, in the first scene, to Buckingham:

> We may outrun
> by violent swiftness that which we run at,
> and lose by overrunning. Know you not
> the fire that mounts the liquor till it run over
> in seeming to augment it wastes it?

The whole first sentence is a pleasure, despite it is another of the old "State" figures speaking, simply that its vocabulary is so dry. It is a most reasonable example of the late verse. As I hear the second line, *the accents* are: "vi", "swift", "that", and "run", in other words not the five feet blank verse goes by. For a good reason: that *the quantity* of the syllables (how long it takes to say them) pulls down the accent to a progress of the line along the length of itself, which progress and which quantities the thinking itself, the idea of outrunning, demands. The quantity asserts itself at once with "by" (long i) and "violent" (not only long i also, but with two following syllables which, though unaccented, are—the long o and the heavy consonantal syllable "lent", 3 consonants to 1 vowel—slow to get through). So much so, in fact, that the first *breath* in the line has here to be taken, even if it is a slight stop before starting to say "swiftness," the "t" on the end of "lent" before the "s" of swiftness requiring the tongue to shift from the upper teethridge (alveolar) off it towards the combined lip and tongue position from which "sw" may be said.

To sum up, then: "by violent" (which is only 1 accent and 4 syllables) already shows forth the weave of accent, quantity, breath which makes prosody the music it is: and here is a very close music, sharp, long and stopped, all in a small space of time, reflecting the truth it is, that this art, when it is at its best, is powerful just because it does obey space-time.

The point of Norfolk's thought is of course to focus the attention on "violent," he is saying to Buckingham that violent running—the fire, overrunning—is what loses the game, spills the energy, wastes it. The music is likewise fit in the rest of the line: "swiftness" itself demands a stop after (the most marked breath the line requires) due to the double-s at its end, as well (reversing the tongue problem between lent and swift) the "th" at the beginning of "that", a tongue-point dental voiced fricative following hard on the voiceless double-s of "ness", also involves the voice in an accent on "that," which here is a relative pronoun opening a clause of some duration—"that which we run at"—which delights because it is so made up of those "necessary shaggy and urban words" Dante called them, the monosyllables comedy can't do without. Which, I should now add, strike me as both what Shakespeare more and more came to depend upon, and for the same reasons, I imagine, that the Americans who now practice the language at something like the same vitality, also depend upon.

I can make this immediate point about Shakespeare's late

verse. It has exactly the characteristic Dante long ago insisted any verse has which places itself back on the vernacular: only two kinds of words have the grandeur right to the deed, the "combed-out" and the "shaggy." The glossy and rumpled won't do. And what does he call the "shaggy" (the combed-out are three syllables, and sweet)? The monosyllables, in other words, the gist of speech; and what he calls the "ornamental poly-syllables," the jaw-breakers, if you like, but for all that the words which hold in themselves the flow and the resistances of feeling, thinking, acting. Dante calls the polysyllables those which, when mixed with combed-out words, produce a "fair harmony of structure" because they have "the roughness of aspirate, accent, double letters, liquids and lengths," in short, breath (aspirate) accent quantity, all three at once, the possibility of same.

One should not have to be bugged because Shakespeare so often does knot up his speech in his late plays, does come up with rough polysyllables, "stops" his lines so much, yields, reluctantly, any of that running-on which made him so suave a poet from *Venus & Adonis* to *Antony & Cleopatra*; and very much doesn't any longer bother to keep his music and thought inside the skin of the person or situation, able as he had been to make each person of his play make his or her individual self register its experience of reality. If the Shakespeare *after* 1607-08 (*Antony & Cleopatra*) is interested instead in making his own thought and music override anybody's, it should only be a sign that he is intending something else than previously, some sort of song other than hers whom he served so long—Erato first, then Melpomene.

That it is now Thalia's song, I come down again on Dante, on another part of his careful analysis of what is possible to comedy. He insists that urban speech alone will do, that "syl-van" won't. (He calls sylvan and urban the two kinds of mas-culine speech there are, delimiting off feminine and child speech as not the business of poets, however much any poet may once have been a child and however as a man he has to listen to women talk.) It is another aspect of these plays, and how long it took Shakespeare to get to them, that they show how much he, and the other Elizabethan poets, were in a dilemma between urban and sylvan by and about Elizabeth's death (1603): though they had exploited London midland speech magnificently in drama, the moment they wanted to do something else, had to do something else, they knew no other mold for it than a sylvan one, the pastoral, than, in fact, that masque which *Comus*, god help us, has been called the triumph of. Is it possible that this sylvan business (which got into England from the Italians of the 16th Century) confounded the very push of urban English? And that only after "Metropolis" —after 300 years, after we have got our fill of urban as city— is it possible to see that Shakespeare sought a form in his late plays which would deliver him from the pastoral and enable him to do what long form has taught us: to be urban at the same time that we are forever rid of "nature," even human "nature," in that damned sylvan sense?

II

In the plays the plots of course, those silly things, *are* pastoral (he hadn't got that far), romantical-pastical, extreme places the events exotic storms floating coffins statues which float a dancing baboon damned countrymen dancing . . . Whoosh. If that were all of it

But something else. Love is pitched where you haven't found it. It is not at all a fluent scene. There are pure awkwardnesses. Women and man say things. My last good deed   You may ride us with one soft kiss a thousand furlongs   It has an elder sister ere with spur we heat an acre   O, would her name were Grace!

> Twenty-three years, and saw myself unbreeched
> in my green velvet coat, my dagger muzzled
> lest it should bite its master and so prove
> (as ornaments often do) too dangerous

> O, then my best blood turn
> And my name with his who did betray the Best!

The delicacy (which would seem the most thing you would say. The scrupulousness

* * * * * * *

The matter is innocence. Innocence, mind you—that it must be kept. An impossible subject. Only a most quiet man, and a very clear one. Without leaving the world as place, to see innocence through it? to do that without, as Lear took it it could only be done out of the world (his Fool died of a cold) in prison? / where he promised Cordelia they would sing and, as God's spies, take upon themselves the mystery of things /. As though only there, one could. It is true, if you are going to leave it at that, at the level of hiring out to God and of a total assignment, the mystery of things.

For a like reason I am not satisfied by the usual insight that the plays are dominated by a search theme, of father for lost child. It sees them from the outside. It looks on them, as the above father and daughter on the world. It makes the error to expect the man, after he has let the world's real sit for portrait, that he will do it again as he had through *Lear* and *Antony & Cleopatra*, that he'll make it so round one can only go aside from it and, as the two do, weep and sing.

"The flatness of my misery!" is what Hermione cries out in the face of what happens to her in *The Winter's Tale*. Each of the three chief classes of people in these new plays—the women, the young, and the fathers—are now forces as statics, and the moving moral or physical dynamics are from those people's own stance, rather than something exerted on them. The one thing which is, is exploded on them, and is the thing they are set, each of them, to offset.

It is in this respect that the plays are best seen as *rites de passage*, in which the poet is making sure, as of these three classes and at three stages, puberty, marriage, and middle life, that, without going aside and at the same time without adding any muscle to overcome the world, outside in its hell or heaven, inside in its heaven or hell, something else is attended to.

At puberty youth is full of protest of the innocence it is

giving up, and because innocence can, at this stage, describe itself, youth gets much voice. The plays, in fact, are an equilibrium between loquacious boys and girls and the terse fathers, with woman the mid term, at once the one who is most sex and most firmed, so much the one who does stand, and stand to it, that the image of her is Hermione who hid from her husband's jealousy and destruction for 19 years and is restored to him, in the end, as a statue out of her own garden!

I shall use Polixenes' description of *the love of boy & boy* but the pairs and their praises of their youth, with flowers the image, are omnipresent—conspicuously Palamon & Arcite in *The Two Noble Kinsmen,* Guiderius and Arviragus the sons of Cymbeline, etc. Polixenes is telling Hermione how it was between him and her husband:

> We were as twinned lambs that did frisk in the sun
> and bleat the one at the other. What we changed
> was innocence for innocence. We knew not
> the doctrine of ill-doing. Nor dreamed
> that any did. Had we pursued that life
> and our weak spirits never been higher reared
> with stronger blood, we should have answered heaven
> boldly, "Not guilty"

The love of man & man is only an extension of the boy thing, and is presented as such, the bond of war replacing tournament and games, and though it does sometimes (as it did earlier in the instance of Coriolanus & Aufidius) nervously admit a simile of marriage, it is to marriage's disadvantage. Hermione, after listening to Polixenes say what he says above, wryly observes: "By this we gather / you have tripped since"!

Against the male thing in the plays Emilia, in *The Two Noble Kinsmen,* directly opposes *the love of girl & girl,* hers, for Flavina. She says to her sister:

> You talk of Pirithous' and Theseus' love.
> Theirs has more ground, is more maturely seasoned,
> more buckled with strong judgment, and their needs
> the one of the other may be said to water
> their intertangled roots of love, but I

and she I sigh and spoke of, were things innocent,
loved for we did, and like the elements . . .

                    What she liked
was then of me approved, what not, condemned

                    The flower that I would pluck
and put between my breasts (then but beginning
to swell about the blossom)

                              On my head no toy
but was her pattern . . .

                    This rehearsal has this end
that the true love between maid and maid may be
more than in sex dividual.

I am saying these ones are not chucks as children were, and
the young pairs of lovers (Perdita-Florizel, Ferdinand-Miranda,
Emilia-Arcite &c) are present as such, neither to be made more
of (Romeo & Juliet) nor to be left as less than the next stage,
marriage, or the further one, middle life. What is so very moving in this new world is the equity. Position, title, the so-called
larger concerns—State passion condition ambition—don't crowd
out something which is less (less in the round world.

Actually, even all that, even the big thing, is, here, made into
a single one, one harsh complication. It is as though suddenly
for Shakespeare Sonnet 129 had rolled up into it all that his
love history and ambition plays amounted to: "The expense of
spirit in a waste of shame / is lust in action and till action lust /
is perjured murderous bloody full of blame / savage extreme
rude cruel not to trust . . ." What is actionable in these plays
follows from lust's outbursts, Leontes', in *The Winter's Tale*,
Iachimo in *Cymbeline*, it breaks in on the noble ones, Palamon
& Arcite, in *Kinsmen*, to split them, it is circumambient in *The
Tempest* where Caliban, the Patagonian, is the danger all the
plays have hidden in them dragged into the light and heaped
up in him as a single carbuncular figure.

Lust is not developmental, it drops, bang, and thus, on this
second level of the action, the plays behave as they do on the
first and third. They are vertical and flat and, as throughout, it

is because it is initiation and not drama which is intended: youth at puberty and the married throughout marriage are seen in a process of finding out how to act to keep what youth had, and age advises, when the fires in the blood flare. Prospero, most the father of the plays, though from Pericles first through Theseus the last there are real or substitute fathers in each, warns Ferdinand, who is about to marry his daughter:

> Do not give dalliance
> too much the rein. The strongest oaths are straw
> to the fire in the blood. Be more abstemious
> or else good night your vow.

The one active principle Shakespeare has, to offer to the uproar of lust, is chastity, which has the root meaning bright, it was originally one with candor, dazzling whiteness, and newfallen snow is Shakespeare's simile. Posthumus, tormented into the conviction his wife has been adulterous, protests she had

> A pudency so rosy the sweet view on it
> might well have warmed old Saturn, that I thought her
> as chaste as unsunned snow

and Ferdinand makes the same comparison of himself as Posthumus of his wife in assuring Prospero

> I warrant you, sir.
> The white cold virgin snow upon my heart
> abates the ardor of my liver.

Youth and woman have this chasteness straight from source, and when innocence is reared, as Polixenes says, "higher," with stronger blood, they do not lose it if they choose not to, to the fires.

I press it (and it is difficult to imagine that it would persuade a modern) because it does seem to be, as of the body of these plays (as it was, to make it more familiar, in *Measure for Measure*) what Shakespeare means to insist upon is the little there is which a man or a woman does have, to wear—as, in the Chinese play, the girl is given by the icy river a cloak which freezes-burns the nobleman who has sought to marry her against her wish, a reverse of Nessus' shirt, in each instance.

42

One may allow it is that way. When you reverse the conclusion of Sonnet 129, when you do oppose the big thing

> All this the world well knows yet none knows well
> to shun the heaven that leads men to this hell

it is bigger, and you are slighter. Your means are slight. Only baffles will do, and the counsel of their use in these plays, as well as their use, comes from what has to be singled out as a third stage of them—what innocence is itself by the rite of its own passage, what is its own regarding that it has known so much it can present boys and girls and men and women, not thrusting about in the foul and terrible exits of the goat world, but proximate, next to themselves, not subdued but equally (as it is another thing one must say of these plays) there are no triumphs. There is only the restoration, no matter at what level in intensity, arbitrary or otherwise, of innocence.

Subject no longer will do. It is also the poet we are now talking about, how he got there that he saw it this way, a way so different it is as though he had walked out of the Renaissance. In one respect he appears not to have at all, in the fierceness with which he fights sensuality as though it were the dogs he so hated who were fed from the tables while the meal was going on. If he seems extreme in this, if he seems as determined as Prospero to keep lust, to keep nature as in an armed camp outside the fence of life, one must now hear the third innocence which falls across the pages of these plays as both their diffidence and a sound just out of hearing. Emilia, in *The Two Noble Kinsmen*, explains herself thus:

> Extremity, that sharpens sundry wits,
> makes me a fool.

It is the question we started from: how the material and means of art, once the Renaissance and its bastard the Modern are passed, are differently disposed and thus the form differently powered.

* * * * * * * *

Winter, he says, winter. Prospero's answer to Miranda's pleasure before the new world she thinks brave—he says, "Tis new to thee"—is no old man's quip. And chastity, it is a sticker a man as post-modern as Lawrence can be no more explicit about (in his last poem to the women who are buried in England whom he has loved) than to asseverate what he says he begged them throughout love, find their virginity.

* * * * * * * *

The question is two things, the attention itself, what it is on (this is most where a change in the discourse system counts); and how it is on, the degree of intensity mounted, that it be the equal of the occasion. It is too frequently unnoticed that it is the former change which makes the latter more likely. There is a great deal of whirlyblade about feeling, about increasing it. But to move the whole stance over, to take a good look at where the in is being sought from . . . There is a rule: a thing ought to take off, and put down, and travel at all the varying speeds in between, precisely equal in amount and behavior to the thing it sets out from or seeks. Or if it multiplies, it only multiplies by changing that thing, not by introducing and asserting outside power (as humanism did and all motors with moving parts do), and the quarrel with it is the waste of energy, which is dispersal and, in the curving about of fact, dispersal comes back and changes, willy-nilly whirligig, the original element of both thing and thing, by making easy the attention and thus reducing the intensity below the level of the implicit power of occasion or of thing.

If the intensity of the attention is equal to it, innocence ought to yield what it is made up of; and when it does, like water in a controlled vacuum, it is enormously *more* than it was in its apparent state. If it is then mixed with what is proper to it (at no point known to me does Shakespeare attack desire) its size and power increase again, and innocence emerges with a thrust much more than sensuality ever gave.

I am suggesting that some such understanding as this is what Shakespeare has reached, and the verse capable of, in these plays. He isn't picking up his objects (words), despite one hand is tied behind his back, either for their music or image. He gets both by going in further to the word as meaning and thing, and, mixing the governing human title and experience (which prompts him to bother with words at all), his effect is the equivalent of his act: the power, instead of peeling off, of being peeled off (as verse and plays had), without being disturbed from its place, twisted into turbulence and action (each not the condition of an element but weather from outside), suddenly moves as one has known it does of its own nature, without using any means or matter other than those local and implicit to it. It is molecular, how this power is, why it all multiplies from itself and from the element proper to its being. We are in the presence of the only truth which the real can have, its own undisclosed because not apparent character. Get that out with no exterior means or materials, no mechanics except those hidden in the thing itself, and we are in the hands of the mystery.

EQUAL, THAT IS,
TO THE REAL ITSELF

Two years before Melville was born John Keats, walking home
from the mummers' play at Christmas 1817, and afterwards,
he'd had to listen to Coleridge again, thought to himself all
that irritable reaching after fact and reason, it won't do. I don't
believe in it. I do better to stay in the condition of things. No
matter what it amounts to, mystery confusion doubt, it has a
power, it is what I mean by *Negative Capability*.

Keats, without setting out to, had put across the century the
inch of steel to wreck Hegel, if anything could. Within five
years, two geometers, Bolyai and Lobatschewsky, weren't any
longer satisfied with Euclid's picture of the world, and they
each made a new one, independently of each other, and remark-
ably alike. It took thirty-one years (Melville's age when he
wrote *Moby-Dick*) for the German mathematician Riemann
to define the real as men since have exploited it: he distinguished two kinds of manifold, the discrete (which would be
the old system, and it includes discourse, language as it had
been since Socrates) and, what he took to be more true, the
continuous.

Melville, not knowing any of this but in it even more as an
American, down to his hips in things, was a first practicer (Rimbaud was born the year Riemann made his inaugural lecture,
1854) of the new equation, quantity as intensive.

The idea on which this book* is based, naturalism, is useless
to cope with Melville, either as a life lived in such a time or

* *The Fine Hammered Steel of Herman Melville*, by Milton R. Stern
(Urbana: University of Illinois Press, 1957).

as an art, the first art of space to arise from the redefinition of the real, and in that respect free, for the first time since Homer, of the rigidities of the discrete. Naturalism was already outmoded by the events above, whether one takes it as an 18th or 19th century idea. Mr. Stern, alas, takes it every way, including the unhappy thought that Melville can be put at the head of a literary use which includes Twain, Dreiser, Hemingway, and Faulkner!

It is the error on matter sitting in naturalism which gives it its appeal, that by it one can avoid the real, which is what is left out, at what cost all over the place Mr. Stern is only one of the fools of. He writes, in summary of what he takes it Melville did prove:

> that the naturalistic perception in the years of the modern could and must take from woe not only materialism but also the humanism and the deep morality of social idealism, which are the true beginnings of wisdom.

The true beginnings of nothing but the Supermarket—the exact death quantity does offer, if it is numbers, and extension, and the appetite of matter, especially in human beings.

The change the 19th century did bring about is being squandered by the 20th, in ignorance and abuse of its truth. Melville was a part of the change, and I can do nothing, in the face of this book, but try to show how, in the terms of that change. He put it altogether accurately himself, in a single sentence of a letter to Hawthorne, written when he was writing *Moby-Dick* (1851): "By visible truth we mean the apprehension of the absolute condition of present things."

All things did come in again, in the 19th century. An idea shook loose, and energy and motion became as important a structure of things as that they are plural, and, by matter, mass. It was even shown that in the infinitely small the older concepts of space ceased to be valid at all. Quantity—the measurable and numerable—was suddenly as shafted in, to any thing, as it was also, as had been obvious, the striking character of the external world, that all things do extend out. Nothing was now inert fact, all things were there for feeling, to promote it, and be felt; and man, in the midst of it, knowing well how he was folded in, as well as how suddenly and strikingly he could extend himself, spring or, without even moving, go, to far, the farthest—he was suddenly possessed or repossessed of a character of being, a thing among things, which I shall call his physicality. It made a reentry of or to the universe. Reality was without interruption, and we are still in the business of finding out how all action, and thought, have to be refounded.

Taking it in towards writing, the discrete, for example, wasn't any longer a good enough base for discourse: classification was exposed as mere taxonomy; and logic (and the sentence as poised on it, a completed thought, instead of what it has become, an exchange of force) was as loose and inaccurate a system as the body and soul had been, divided from each other and rattling, sticks in a stiff box.

Something like this are the terms of the real and of action Melville was an early inheritor of, and he is either held this way or he is missed entirely. With one thing more: the measurement question. What did happen to measure when the rigidities dissolved? When Newton's Scholium turned out to be the fulling-mill Melville sensed it was, via Bacon, whom he called that watch-maker brain? What is measure when the universe flips and no part is discrete from another part except by the flow of creation itself, in and out, intensive where it seemed before qualitative, and the extensive exactly the widest, which we also have the powers to include? Rhythm, suddenly, which had been so long the captive of meter, no matter how good (Shakespeare, say, in our own tongue, or Chaucer), was a pumping of the real so constant art had to invent measure anew.

Watching Melville in a lifetime trying to make prose do what his body and his soul as a heap, and his mind on top of them a tangle (this is also a way of putting a man's physicality), trying to get a measure of language to move himself into a book and over to another man's experience, is a study makes more sense now, in the midst of 20th century art, painting and music as well as narrative and verse, than it could have, previously. It wasn't image, it wasn't anything he lacked. Possibly it was only any reason he might be confident he was right, taking it all so differently as he did, from those around him, at least those known to him. Or say it as my friend Landreau does, who swings, with *The Confidence-Man*: "Melville seems entitled to 'disillusion itself,' and given his personal bitter life, possibly because of that vision, in the scene, society, he had to live it in."

Who still knows what's called for, from physicality, how far it does cover and reveal? No one has yet tried to say how Melville does manage to give the flukes of the whale immediacy as such. It is easier to isolate his skill over technology than to investigate the topological both in his soul and in his writing, but it is my experience that only some such sense or form as the topological includes, able to discriminate and get in between the vague *types* of form morphology offers and the *ideal* structures of geometry proper, explains Melville's unique ability to reveal the very large (such a thing as his whale, or himself on whiteness, or Ahab's monomania) by the small.

The new world of atomism offered a metrical means as well as a topos different from the discrete. Congruence, which there, in mathematicians' hands, lifted everything forward after Lobatschewsky (via Cayley especially, another contemporary of Melville, and Felix Klein) makes much sense, as no other meter does, to account for Melville's prose. Congruence was spatial intuition to Kant, and if I am right that Melville did possess its powers, he had them by his birth, from his time of the world, locally America. As it developed in his century, congruence, which had been the measure of the space a solid fills in two of its positions, became a point-by-point mapping power of such flexibility that anything which stays the same, no matter where it goes and into whatever varying conditions (it can suffer deformation), it can be followed, and, if it is art, led, including, what is so important to prose, such physical quantities as velocity, force and field strength.

Melville's prose does things which its rhetoric would seem to contradict. He manages almost any time he wants to, for example, to endow a more general space than other writers, than anyone except Homer I find. The delivery of Tashtego from the whale's head, say. The point is also the overall "space" of *Moby-Dick*. That space, and those of which it is made up, have the properties of projective space (otherwise they should all come out more familiar, and round, because they would stay Euclidean), and I conclude that Melville could not have achieved what amounts to elliptical and hyperbolic spaces (he makes things stand out at once transparent and homogeneous) if he were not using transformations which we have not understood and which only congruence makes possible. (The lack of it, in his verse, as negativism in his life, such as Keats knew, is one of the ways of putting how far Melville *didn't* go.)

His ideas also. In spite of the vocabulary of his time, much more is to be read out of him, I suspect, than any of us have allowed. In the rest of the letter to Hawthorne from which I have quoted, he goes on to discuss the effects of the absolute of present things on self, and being, and God and his insistence there, to get God in the street, looks to me like the first rate breakthrough of man's thought which was called for at 1851: the necessary secularization of His part in the world of things. (It doesn't diminish it, that it was probably the only time in a lifetime in which Melville did manage to throw off the Semitic notion of transcendence.)

Or take him just where so much academicism has wasted its time on classic American literature, and Mr. Stern does again: the place of allegory and symbol in Melville and his contemporaries. As the Master said to me in the dream, of rhythm is image / of image is knowing / of knowing there is / a construct. It is rather quantum physics than relativity which will supply a proper evidence here, as against naturalism, of what Melville was grabbing on to when he declared it was *visible* truth he was after. For example, that light is not only a wave but a corpuscle. Or that the electron is not only a corpuscle but a wave. Melville couldn't abuse object as symbol does by depreciating it in favor of subject. Or let image lose its relational force by transferring its occurrence as allegory does. It was already aware of the complementarity of each of two pairs of how we know and present the real—image & object, and action & subject—both of which have paid off so decisively since. At this end I am thinking of such recent American painting as Pollock's, and Kline's, and some recent American narrative and verse; and at his end, his whale itself for example, what an unfolding thing it is as it sits there written 100 years off, implicit intrinsic and incident to itself.

Melville was not tempted, as Whitman was, and Emerson and Thoreau differently, to inflate the physical: take the model for the house, the house for the model, death is the open road, the soul or body is a boat, etc. Melville equally couldn't spiritualize it, as Hawthorne tried, using such sets as the mirror image, M. de Miroir, etc., and Melville himself in *The Bell Tower*, but not in *The Encantadas*, or *Bartleby*, and how explain the way the remark "The negro" does hold off and free in *Benito Cereno?* Melville wouldn't have known it to say it this way, but he was essentially incapable of either allegory or symbol for the best of congruent reason: mirror and model are each figures in Euclidean space, and they are *not* congruent. They require a discontinuous jump.

Finally, to take the possibilities here suggested, at their fullest—the actual character and structure of the real itself. I pick up on calm, or passivity, Melville's words, and about which he knew something, having served as a boatsteerer himself, on at least his third voyage on a whaler in the Pacific. He says somewhere a harpoon can only be thrown accurately from such repose as he also likened the White Whale to, as it finally approached, a mighty mildness of repose in swiftness is his phrase. Likewise, in handling Ahab's monomania, he sets up a different sort of a possible man, one of a company which he calls the hustings of the Divine Inert.

I am able to stress the several aspects of Melville's thought on this because, note, in each case the feeling or necessity of the inert, or of passivity as a position of rest, is joined to the most instant and powerful actions Melville can invent: the whale itself's swiftness, Ahab's inordinate will, and the harpooneer's ability to strike to kill from calm only. *The inertial structure of the world is a real thing which not only exerts effects upon matter but in turn suffers such effects.*

I don't know a more relevant single fact to the experience of *Moby-Dick* and its writer than this. Unless it is the prior and lesser but more characteristic Riemannian observation, that the metrical structure of the world is so intimately connected to the inertial structure that the metrical field (art is measure) will of necessity become flexible (what we are finding out these days in painting writing and music) the moment the inertial field itself is flexible.

Which it is, Einstein established, by the phenomena of gravitation, and the dependence of the field of inertia on matter. I take care to be inclusive, to enforce the point made at the start, that matter offers perils wider than man if he doesn't do what still today seems the hardest thing for him to do, outside of some art and science: to believe that things, and present ones, are the absolute conditions; but that they are so because the structures of the real are flexible, quanta do dissolve into vibrations, all does flow, and yet is there, to be made permanent, if the means are equal.

HUMAN UNIVERSE

There are laws, that is to say, the human universe is as discoverable as that other. And as definable.

The trouble has been, that a man stays so astonished he can triumph over his own incoherence, he settles for that, crows over it, and goes at a day again happy he at least makes a little sense. Or if he says anything to another, he thinks it is enough—the struggle does involve such labor and some terror—to wrap it in a little mystery: ah, the way is hard but this is what you find if you go it.

The need now is a cooler one, a discrimination, and then, a shout. Der Weg stirbt, sd one. And was right, was he not? Then the question is: was ist der Weg?

I

The difficulty of discovery (in the close world which the human is because it is ourselves and nothing outside us, like the other) is, that definition is as much a part of the act as is sensation itself, in this sense, that life *is* preoccupation with itself, that conjecture about it is as much of it as its coming at us, its going on. In other words, we are ourselves both the instrument of discovery and the instrument of definition.

Which is of course, why language is a prime of the matter and why, if we are to see some of the laws afresh, it is necessary to examine, first, the present condition of the language—and I mean language exactly in its double sense of discrimination (logos) and of shout (tongue).

We have lived long in a generalizing time, at least since 450 B.C. And it has had its effects on the best of men, on the best of things. Logos, or discourse, for example, has, in that time, so worked its abstractions into our concept and use of language that language's other function, speech, seems so in need of restoration that several of us go back to hieroglyphs or to ideograms to right the balance. (The distinction here is between language as the act of the instant and language as the act of thought about the instant.)

But one can't any longer, stop there, if one ever could. For the habits of thought are the habits of action, and here, too, particularism has to be fought for, anew. In fact, by the very law of the identity of definition and discovery, who can extricate language from action? (Though it is one of the first false faces of the law which I shall want to try to strike away, it is quite understandable—in the light of this identity—that the Greeks went on to declare all speculation as enclosed in the "UNIVERSE of discourse." It is their word, and the refuge of all metaphysicians since—as though language, too, was an absolute, instead of (as even man is) instrument, and not to be extended, however much the urge, to cover what each, man and language, is in the hands of: what we share, and which is enough, of power and of beauty, not to need an exaggeration of words, especially that spreading one, "universe." For discouse is hardly such, or at least only arbitrarily a universe. In any case, so extended (logos given so much more of its part than live speech), discourse has arrogated to itself a good deal of experience which needed to stay put—needs now to be returned to the only two universes which count, the two phenomenal ones, the two a man has need to bear on because they bear so on him: that of himself, as organism, and that of his environment, the earth and planets.

We stay unaware how two means of discourse the Greeks appear to have invented hugely intermit our participation in our experience, and so prevent discovery. They are what followed from Socrates' readiness to generalize, his willingness (from his own bias) to make a "universe" out of discourse instead of letting it rest in its most serviceable place. (It is not sufficiently observed that logos, and the reason necessary to it, are only a stage which a man must master and not what they are taken to be, final discipline. Beyond them is direct perception and the contraries which dispose of argument. The harmony of the universe, and I include man, is not logical, or better, is post-logical, as is the order of any created thing.) With Aristotle, the two great means appear: logic and classification. And it is they that have so fastened themselves on habits of thought that action is interfered with, absolutely interfered with, I should say.

Nor can I let the third of the great Greeks, Plato, go free— he who had more of a sort of latitude and style my tribe of men are apt to indulge him for. His world of Ideas, of forms as extricable from content, is as much and as dangerous an issue as are logic and classification, and they need to be seen as such if we are to get on to some alternative to the whole Greek system. Plato may be a honey-head, as Melville called him, but he is precisely that—treacherous to all ants, and where, increasingly, my contemporaries die, or drown the best of themselves. Idealisms of any sort, like logic and like classification, intervene at just the moment they become more than the means they are, are allowed to become ways as end instead of ways *to* end, END, which is never more than this instant, than you on this instant, than you, figuring it out, and acting, so. If there is any absolute, it is never more than this one, you, this instant, in action.

Which ought to get us on. What makes most acts—of living and of writing—unsatisfactory, is that the person and/or the writer satisfy themselves that they can only make a form (what they say or do, or a story, a poem, whatever) by selecting from the full content some face of it, or plane, some part. And at just this point, by just this act, they fall back on the dodges of discourse, and immediately, they lose me, I am no longer engaged, this is not what I know is the going-on (and of which going-on I, as well as they, want some illumination, and so, some pleasure). It comes out a demonstration, a separating out, an act of classification, and so, a stopping, and all that I know is, it is not there, it has turned false. For any of us, at any instant, are juxtaposed to any experience, even an overwhelming single one, on several more planes than the arbitrary and discursive which we inherit can declare.

It is not the Greeks I blame. What it comes to is ourselves, that we do not find ways to hew to experience as it is, in our definition and expression of it, in other words, find ways to stay in the human universe, and not be led to partition reality at any point, in any way. For this is just what we do do, this is the real issue of what has been, and the process, as it now asserts itself, can be exposed. It is the function, *comparison*, or, its bigger name, *symbology*. These are the false faces, too much seen, which hide and keep from use the active intellectual states, metaphor and performance, All that comparison ever does is set up a series of *reference* points: to compare is to take one thing and try to understand it by marking its similarities to or differences from another thing. Right here is the trouble, that each thing is not so much like or different from another thing (these likenesses and differences are apparent) but that such an analysis only accomplishes a *description*, does not come to grips with what really matters: that a thing, any thing, impinges on us by a more important fact, its self-existence, without reference to any other thing, in short, the very character of it which calls our attention to it, which wants us to know more about it, its particularity. This is what we are confronted by, not the thing's "class," any hierarchy, of quality or quantity, but the thing itself, and its *relevance* to ourselves who are the experience of it (whatever it may mean to someone else, or whatever other relations it may have).

There must be a means of expression for this, a way which is not divisive as all the tag ends and upendings of the Greek way are. There must be a way which bears *in* instead of away, which meets head on what goes on each split second, a way which does not—in order to define—prevent, deter, distract, and so cease the act of, discovering.

I have been living for some time amongst a people who are more or less directly the descendants of a culture and a civilization which was a contrary of that which we have known and of which we are the natural children. The marked thing about them is, that it is only love and flesh which seems to carry any sign of their antecedence, that all the rest which was once a

56

greatness different from our own has gone down before the poundings of our way. And, now, except as their bodies jostle in a bus, or as they disclose the depth and tenacity of love among each other inside a family, they are poor failures of the modern world, incompetent even to arrange that, in the month of June, when the rains have not come far enough forward to fill the wells, they have water to wash in or to drink. They have lost the capacity of their predecessors to do anything in common. But they do one thing no modern knows the secret of, however he is still by nature possessed of it: they wear their flesh with that difference which the understanding that it is common leads to. When I am rocked by the roads against any of them—kids, women, men—their flesh is most gentle, is granted, touch is in no sense anything but the natural law of flesh, there is none of that pull-away which, in the States, causes a man for all the years of his life the deepest sort of questioning of the rights of himself to the wild reachings of his own organism. The admission these people give me and one another is direct, and the individual who peers out from that flesh is precisely himself, is a curious wandering animal like me—it is so very beautiful how animal human eyes are when the flesh is not worn so close it chokes, how human and individuated the look comes out of a human eye when the house of it is not exaggerated.

This is not easy to save from subjectivism, to state so that you understand that this is not an observation but a first law to a restoration of the human house. For what is marked about these Lermeros with whom I live (by contrast, for example, to the people of the city nearby) is that, here, the big-eared, small-eyed creatures stay as the minority they must always have been before garages made them valuable and allowed them out of their holes to proliferate and overrun the earth. Nothing is accident, and man, no less than nature, does nothing without plan or the discipline to make plan fact. And if it is true that we now live in fear of our own house, and can easily trace the reason for it, it is also true that we can trace reasons why those who do not or did not so live found out how to do other than we.

My assumption is, that these contemporary Maya are what they are because once there was a concept at work which kept attention so poised that (1) men were able to stay so interested in the expression and gesture of all creatures, including at least three planets in addition to the human face, eyes and hands, that they invented a system of written record, now called hiero-glyphs, which, on its very face, is verse, the signs were so clearly and densely chosen that, cut in stone, they retain the power of the objects of which they are the images; (2) to mass stone with sufficient proportion to decorate a near hill and turn it into a firetower or an observatory or one post of an enclosure in which people, favored by its shadows, might swap caymotes for san-dals; and (3) to fire clay into pots porous enough to sieve and thus cool water, strong enough to stew iguana and fish, and handsome enough to put ceremony where it also belongs, in the most elementary human acts. And when a people are so dis-posed, it should come as no surprise that, long before any of these accomplishments, the same people did an improvement on nature—the domestication of maize—which remains one of the world's wonders, even to a nation of Burbanks, and that long after all their accomplishments, they still carry their bodies with some of the savor and the flavor that the bodies of the Ameri-cans are as missing in as is their irrigated lettuce and their green-picked refrigerator-ripened fruit. For the truth is, that the management of external nature so that none of its virtu is lost, in vegetables or in art, is as much a delicate juggling of her content as is the same juggling by any one of us of our own. And when men are not such jugglers, are not able to manage a means of expression the equal of their own or nature's intricacy, the flesh does choke. The notion of fun comes to displace work as what we are here for. Spectatorism crowds out participation as the condition of culture. And bonuses and prizes are the re-wards of labor contrived by the monopolies of business and government to protect themselves from the advancement in position of able men or that old assertion of an inventive man, his own shop. All individual energy and ingenuity is bought off—at a suggestion box or the cinema. Passivity conquers all.

Even war and peace die (to be displaced by world government?) and man reverts to only two of his components, inertia and gas. It is easy to phrase, too easy, and we have had enough of bright description. To say that in America the goods are as the fruits, and the people as the goods, all glistening but tasteless, accomplishes nothing in itself, for the overwhelming fact is, that the rest of the world wants nothing but to be the same. Value is perishing from the earth because no one cares to fight down to it beneath the glowing surfaces so attractive to all. Der Weg stirbt.

II

Can one restate man in any way to repossess him of his dynamic? I don't know. But for myself a first answer lies in his systemic particulars. The trouble with the inherited formulations which have helped to destroy him (the notion of himself as the center of phenomenon by fiat or of god as the center and man as god's chief reflection)is that both set aside nature as an unadmitted or suppressed third party, a sort of Holy Ghost which was allowed in once to touch men's tongues and then, because the fire was too great, was immediately banished to some sort of half place in between god and the devil—who actually, of course, thereby became the most powerful agent of all. The result, we have been the witnesses of: discovering this discarded thing nature, has run away with everything. Tapping her power, fingering her like a child, giving her again her place, but without somehow, remembering what truth there was in man's centering the use of anything, god, devil, or holy ghost, in himself, science has upset all balance and blown value, man's peculiar responsibility, to the winds.

If unselectedness is man's original condition (such is more accurate a word than that lovely riding thing, chaos, which sounds like what it is, the most huge generalization of all, obviously making it necessary for man to invent a bearded giant to shape it for him) but if likewise, selectiveness is just as originally the impulse by which he proceeds to do something about the unselectedness, then one is forced, is one not, to look for some instrumentation in man's given which makes selection possible. And it has gone so far, that is, science has, as to wonder if the fingertips, are not very knowing knots in their own rights, little brains (little photo-electric cells, I think they now call the skin) which, immediately, in responding to external stimuli, make decisions! It is a remarkable and usable idea. For it is man's first cause of wonder how rapid he is in his taking in of what he does experience.

But when you have said that, have you not done one of two things, either forever damned yourself by making the "soul" mechanical (it has long been the soul which has softly stood as a word to cover man as a selecting internal reality posed dangerously in the midst of those externals which the word chaos generously covers like Williams' paint) or you have possibly committed a greater crime. You have allowed that external reality is more than merely the substance which man takes in. By making the threshold of reception so important and by putting the instrumentation of selection so far out from its traditional place (the greatest humanist of them all opened a sonnet, "Poor soul, the centre of my sinful earth"), you have gone so far as to imply that the skin itself, the meeting edge of man and external reality, is where all that matters does happen, that man and external reality are so involved with one another that, for man's purposes, they had better be taken as one.

It is some such crime by which I am willing to hazard a guess at a way to restore to man some of his lost relevance. For this metaphor of the senses—of the literal speed of light by which a man absorbs, instant on instant, all that phenomenon presents to him—is a fair image as well, my experience tells me, of the ways of his inner energy, of the ways of those other things which are usually, for some reason, separated from the external pick-ups—his dreams, for example, his thoughts (to speak as the predecessors spoke), his desires, sins, hopes, fears, faiths, loves. I am not able to satisfy myself that these so-called inner things are so separable from the objects, persons, events which are the content of them and by which man represents or re-enacts them despite the suck of symbol which has increased and increased since the great Greeks first promoted the idea of a transcendent world of forms. What I do see is that each man does make his own special selection from the phenomenal field, and it is thus that we begin to speak of personality, however I remain unaware that this particular act of individuation is peculiar to man, observable as it is in individuals of other species of nature's making (it behooves man now not to separate himself too jauntily from any of nature's creatures).

Even if one does follow personality up, does take the problem further in to those areas of function which may seem more peculiarly human (at least are more peculiarly the concern of a humanist), I equally cannot satisfy myself of the gain in thinking that the process by which man transposes phenomenon to his use is any more extricable from reception than reception itself is from the world. What happens at the skin is more like than different from what happens within. The process of image (to be more exact about transposition than the "soul" allows or than the analysts do with their tricky "symbol-maker") cannot be understood by separation from the stuff it works on. Here again, as throughout experience, the law remains, form is not isolated from content. The error of all other metaphysic is descriptive, is the profound error that Heisenberg had the intelligence to admit in his principle that a thing can be measured in its mass only by arbitrarily assuming a stopping of its motion, or in its motion only by neglecting, for the moment of the measuring, its mass. And either way, you are failing to get what you are after—so far as a human being goes, his life. There is only one thing you can do about kinetic, reenact it. Which is why the man said, he who possesses rhythm possesses the universe. And why art is the only twin life has—its only valid metaphysic. Art does not seek to describe but to enact. And if man is once more to possess intent in his life, and to take up the responsibility implicit in his life, he has to comprehend his own process as intact, from outside, by way of his skin, in, and by his own powers of conversion, out again. For there is this other part of the motion which we call life to be examined anew, that thing we overlove, man's action, that tremendous discharge of force which we overlove when we love it for its own sake but which (when it is good) is the equal of all intake plus all transposing.

It deserves this word, that it is the equal of its cause only when it proceeds unbroken from the threshold of a man through him and back out again, without loss of quality, to the external world from which it came, whether that external world take the shape of another human being or of the several human beings hidden by the generalization "society" or of things themselves. In other words, the proposition here is that man at his peril breaks the full circuit of object, image, action at any point. The meeting edge of man and the world is also his cutting edge. If man is active, it is exactly here where experience comes in that it is delivered back, and if he stays fresh at the coming in he will be fresh at his going out. If he does not, all that he does inside his house is stale, more and more stale as he is less and less acute at the door. And his door is where he is responsible to more than himself. Man does influence external reality, and it can be stated without recourse to the stupidities of mysticism (which appears to love a mystery as much outside as it does in). If man chooses to treat external reality any differently than as part of his own process, in other words as anything other than relevant to his own inner life, then he will (being such a froward thing, and bound to use his energy willy-nilly, nature is so subtle) use it otherwise. He will use it just exactly as he has used it now for too long, for arbitrary and willful purposes which, in their effects, not only change the face of nature but actually arrest and divert her force until man turns it even against herself, he is so powerful, this little thing. But what little willful modern man will not recognize is, that when he turns it against her he turns it against himself, held in the hand of nature as man forever is, to his use of himself if he choose, to his disuse, as he has.

What gets me is, how man refuses to acknowledge the consequences of his disposing of himself at his own entrance—as though a kiss were a cheap thing, as though he were. He will give a Rimbaud a lot of lip and no service at all, as though Rimbaud were a sport of nature and not a proof. Or a people different from himself—they will be the subject of historians' studies or of tourists' curiosity, and be let go at that, no matter how much they may disclose values he and his kind, you would think, could make use of. I have found, for example, that the hieroglyphs of the Maya disclose a placement of themselves toward nature of enormous contradiction to ourselves, and yet I am not aware that any of the possible usages of this difference have been allowed to seep out into present society. All that is done is what a Toynbee does, diminish the energy once here expended into the sieve phonetic words have become to be offered like one of nature's pastes that we call jewels to be hung as a decoration of knowledge upon some Christian and therefore eternal and holy neck. It is unbearable what knowledge of the past has been allowed to become, what function of human memory has been dribbled out to in the hands of these learned monsters whom people are led to think "know." They know nothing in not knowing how to reify what they do know. What is worse, they do not know how to pass over to us the energy implicit in any high work of the past because they purposely destroy that energy as dangerous to the states for which they work—which it is, for any concrete thing is a danger to rhetoricians and politicians, as dangerous as a hard coin is to a banker. And the more I live the more I am tempted to think that the ultimate reason why man departs from nature and thus departs from his own chance is that he is part of a herd which wants to do the very thing which nature disallows—that energy can be lost. When I look at the filth and lumber which man is led by, I see man's greatest achievement in this childish accomplishment—that he damn well can, and does, destroy destroy destroy energy every day. It is too much. It is too much to waste time on, this idiot who spills his fluids like some truculent and fingerless chamaco hereabouts who wastes water at the pump when birds are dying all over the country in this hottest of the months and women come in droves in the morning begging for even a tasa of the precious stuff to be poured in the amphoras they swing on their hips as they swing their babies. Man has made himself an ugliness and a bore.

It was better to be a bird, as these Maya seem to have been, they kept moving their heads so nervously to stay alive, to keep alerted to what they were surrounded by, to watch it even for the snake they took it to be or that larger bird they had to be in awe of, the zopalote who fed on them when they were dead or whom they looked at of a morning in a great black heap like locusts tearing up a deer had broken his wind or leg in the night. Or even Venus they watched, as though they were a grackle themselves and could attack her vertically in her house full of holes like a flute through which, they thought, when she had the upper hand she spread down on them, on an east wind, disease and those blows on their skin they call granitos. When she was new, when she buzzed the morning sky, they hid in their houses for fear of her, Shoosh Ek, for fear of her bite, the Wasp she was, the way she could throw them down like that electrical stick which, last year, pinched one of these fishermen on his cheek, in all the gulf hit him as he sat in the prow of his cayuco with a line out for dogfish of a day and laid him out dead, with no more mark burned on him than that little tooth of a kiss his wife was given as cause when they brought him out over the beach as he might have hauled in a well-paying shark.

Or to be a man and a woman as Sun was, the way he had to put up with Moon, from start to finish the way she was, the way she behaved, and he up against it because he did have the the advantage of her, he moved more rapidly. In the beginning he was only young and full of himself, and she, well, she was a girl living with her grandfather doing what a girl was supposed to be doing, making cloth. Even then he had the advantage of her, he hunted, instead, and because he could hunt he could become a humming-bird, which he did, just to get closer to her, this loveliness he thought she was and wanted to taste. Only the trouble was, he had to act out his mask, and while he was coming closer, one tobacco flower to another toward the house, her grandfather brought him down with a clay shot from a blow gun. And sun fell, right into moon's arms, who took him to her room to mother him, for she was already to be a wife, a man's second mother as a wife is in these parts where birds are so often stoned and need to be brought back to consciousness and, if they have their wings intact, may fly away again. As sun was. Only he could also talk, and persuaded moon to elope with him in a canoe. But there you are: there is always danger. Grandfather gets rain to throw his fire at them and though sun converts to turtle and is tough enough to escape alive, moon, putting on a crab shell, is not sufficiently protected and is killed.

Which is only part of it, that part of it which is outside and seems to have all of the drama. But only seems. For dragonflies collect moon's flesh and moon's blood in thirteen hollow logs, the sort of log sun had scooped his helpless runaway boat out of, thinking he had made it, had moon finally for his own. Foolish sun. For now here he is back again, after thirteen days, digging out the thirteen logs, and finding that twelve of them contain nothing but all the insects and all the snakes which fly and crawl about the earth of man and pester people in a hot climate so that a lot die off before they are well begun and most are ready, at any instant, for a sickness or a swelling, and the best thing to do is to lie quiet, wait for the poison to pass. For there is log 13, and it reveals moon restored to life, only moon is missing that part which makes woman woman, and deer alone, deer can give her what he does give her so that she and sun can do what man and woman have the pleasure to do as one respite from the constant hammering.

But you see, nothing lasts. Sun has an older brother, who comes to live with sun and moon, and sun has reason soon to suspect that something is going on between moon and the big star, for this brother is the third one of the sky, the devilish or waspish one who is so often with moon. By a trick, sun discovers them, and moon, dispirited, sitting off by herself on the river bank, is persuaded by the bird zopalote to go off with him to the house of the king of the vultures himself. And though a vulture is not, obviously, as handsome a thing as the sun, do not be fooled into thinking that this bird which can darken the sky as well as feed on dead things until they are only bones for the sun to whiten, has not his attractions, had not his attractions to moon, especially the king of them all. She took him, made him the third of her men, and was his wife.

But sun was not done with her, with his want of her, and he turned to that creature which empowered her, the deer, for aid. He borrowed a skin, and hiding under it—knowing as hot sun does the habits of vultures—he pretends to be a carcass. The first vulture comes in, landing awkwardly a distance off, hobbles his nervous way nearer until, as he is about to pick apart what he thinks is a small deer, sun leaps on his back and rides off to where moon is. He triumphantly seizes her, only to find that she is somewhat reluctant to return.

At which stage, for reasons of cause or not, sun and moon go up into the sky to assume forever their planetary duties. But sun finds there is one last thing he must do to the moon before human beings are satisfied with her. He must knock out one of her eyes, they complain she is so bright and that they cannot sleep, the night is so much the same as his day, and his day is too much anyhow, and a little of the sweetness of the night they must have. So he does, he puts out her eye, and lets human beings have what they want. But when he does more, when, occasionally, he eclipses her entirely, some say it is only a sign that the two of them continue to fight, presumably because sun cannot forget moon's promiscuity, though others say that moon is forever erratic, is very much of a liar, is always telling sun about the way people of the earth are as much misbehavers as she, get drunk, do the things she does, in fact, the old ones say, moon is as difficult to understand as any bitch is.

O, they were hot for the world they lived in, these Maya, hot to get it down the way it was—the way it is, my fellow citizens. ⁻

II

The following selection of letters is taken from those written to the editor when Olson was living in Lerma at the tip of the Yucatan peninsula, close to Campeche and Merida. He was there, roughly, six months. In editing the letters I have tried to maintain a continuity, and have indicated excisions with dots (. . .), whenever such were necessary.   R.C.

MAYAN LETTERS

1

saturday feb 18 (is it?)   lerma, campeche, mexico

Birds, lad: my god what birds. Last evening a thing like our hawk. And that woman of mine (again) most alert to their nature. It happened this way. I was down the beach bargaining to buy a piece of their best fish here, what sounds like madrigal, only it comes out smedreegal. I had my back turned no more than three minutes, when, turning, to come back to the house (Con was on the terraza out over the sea, surrounded by a dozen of these gabbling kids), below her, on the water line, I noticed these huge wings fluttering wrong. My guess was, one of the kids, all of whom carry sling-shots, had brought down a zopalote (our vulture, "brother v," as Con named them). But when I came near, I noticed, just as Con cried down, that it was no vulture but another bird which is quite beautiful here, in Maya a chii-mi (chee-me): flies in flock over the waterline, soaring like hawks, high, and is marked by a long splittail ((by god, i was right : just checked dictionary, and is, as I thought, our frigate bird))

there it was, poor chii-mi, stoned by one of these little bastards, and the others, throwing more stones at it, and a couple, kicking it. And it working those three foot wings, hard, but not wild: very sure of itself, tho downed. By the time I came up, it had managed to get itself over, and was already out into the water, to get away from the kids. But each wave was wetting it down, and the misery was, that it drown.

My assumption was, the stone had broken its wing. But Con had seen it happen, and seems to have known it was only its head that had been struck (it was out cold, she told me later, for a minute or so, and then, on its back, had disgorged its last fish). Anyhow, she had the brains to send down one of the older boys to bring it out of the water, and up on the terraza. And when I came up, there it was, quiet, looking hard at everyone, with its gular pouch swollen like my Aunt Vandla's goiter, and its eye, not at all as a bird's is, when it is scared, or as, so quickly, they weaken, and that film drops over the eye. Not at all: this chii-mi was more like an animal, in its strength. Yet I still thought it was done for, something in the wings gone.

Just about then it started to work its way forward, pulling its wings in to its body, and making it look so much more like, say, a duck. What it had in mind, was to try to lift itself the two feet up to the wall that goes round the terraza. But it could not. It had worked itself into the inner angle of a corner. So I reached down and raised the right wing up to the top of the wall. Then the left. And, itself, it pulled its body up, perched for an instant, and swung off, off and up, into the sky, god help us, up and out over the sea, higher and higher, and, not like the others but working its wings in shorter, quicker strokes, it pulled off and off, out over the shrimp ship moored out in the deeper water, inside the bar, from which it swung inland again, and, as I watched it a good five minutes, kept turning more and more to the west, into the sun, until that peculiar movement of the wings began to give way to the more usual flight of a chii-mi. And I figure, as it disappeared, it was all right, all right.

God, it was wonderful, black, wonderful long feathers, and the wing spread, overall, what, five to six feet. Never got such a sense of a bird's strength, inside strength, as this one gave, like I say, more animal, seemingly, and sure, none of that small beating heart. That's why its victory, over these mean little pricks, was so fine.

(Its silhouette, anyway, above us each day, is a lovely thing, the fore part of the wing not a curve as in a gull, but angled like a bat's a third out from the body. And this strange double tail splitting in flight like the steepest sort of an arrow.

How come "chii-mi" I can't yet tell you, though, last night, in my Dictionario Motul, which arrived yesterday from Merida and gives me a fair start in to the ride of this Maya tongue, I was able to locate "chii," as "margin" of the sea, a page, a dress, etcetera. "Mi" I still can't find in the proliferation of double consonants, double vowels, and five extra letters beyond Western alphabets (I daresay if I had Tozzer's Maya-English dictionary (the only one, I now learn), I'd be better off. To try to find anything through the screen of one unknown language to another! (this D. Motul is the base work, Maya-Espanol, done here in the Yucatan mid-16th century, and not equalled since. My edition is by the one Mexican scholar whom I have yet had occasion to raise respect for, a 82 yr old citizen named Juan Martínez Hernández.) . . .

But I've been happier, by an act of circumvention, the last three days: I have been in the field, away from people, working around stones in the sun, putting my hands in to the dust and fragments and pieces of those Maya who used to live here down and along this road.

And the joy is, the whole area within the easiest walking distances, is covered with their leavings: I already have in front of me as I write to you the upper half of an owl idol's (?) head, which I picked up on a farm five minutes from the house! And two half plates, among other fragments of pots, quite fine in the working of the clay, though the painting is average.

The big thing, tho, is the solidity of the sense of their lives one can get right here in the fields and on the hill which rises quite steeply from the shore. Thursday afternoon Con and I went back in, say, five miles, and ran into something which would take the top off yr head: on the highest hill, looking out over a savannah which runs straight and flat to the sea here, a sort of farm moor (it was maize once, but, due to the way of Mayan agriculture, grass defeated corn inside of seven years, and from then on, the grass is so durable, neither forest nor corn can come again), on that hill where the sea's winds reach, where the overlook is so fine, these Maya had once built what appears to have been a little city. I say appears, for now, after six years of the Sanchez Construction Co. crushing the stones of that city, we were able to see only one piece of one column of what (the Indian workers told us) was once, six years ago, many many such columns *in place!* (The whole experience was like the deserts we found in and around Sacramento, where the gold Companies have, with their huge water shitting machines, spoiled the earth (in this case not men's work, but nature's soil accumulation, for ever, mind you, forever: they turn the top soil down under and pile on top of it, as their crawling machine goes along, all the crunched gravel and stone their water-test has proven not to contain gold, or the dust, of gold)

Crazy, "stupido," as the Indians at least, know it to be: it angers me two ways (1) that the rubble beneath the facings, columns, worked facades, etc., is the bulk of the stone, and there is no reason except laziness, that the worked things, so small a part of the whole, should not have been set aside; and (2) that this is the laziness, not of Sanchez & Co., which one has to grant its stupidity, but is the stupidity & laziness of the archaeologists, both American & Mexican, which is that most culpable of all, intellectual carelessness.

I had the feeling, already in Merida, that the Peabody-Carnegie gang, whatever they may have done, 50, or 25 years ago, were, now, missing the job, were typical pedants or academics, and were playing some state & low professional game. Like this: that, at this date, it was no longer so important to uncover buried cities and restore same, as it was to strike in anew by two paths: (1) what I have already sounded off to you about, the living Maya language and what its perdurables, because language is so tough, may well contain in the heads of these living farmers back one block, from this street, or wherever, the deeper in, I imagine, the more and (2) in the present context the important one: a total reconnaissance of *all* sites (laugh as they did at me in Merida, the "experts") instead of (as the Carnegie-Mexican Govt is about to launch) the recovery of the 3rd of the Maya Metropolises here in the peninsula, Mayapan.

The joker is, they are "advanced" enough to justify the Mayapan operation as a step to discover more abt the economic & political life of the ancient Maya! Which, of course, kills me. Here I am an aestheticist (which I have yet to be convinced *any* one of them, from Stephens on down, is). And now, when they, these professionals, are catching on (EP's 35 yr lag, surely), to the validity of the total life of a people as what cargo art discharges, I am the one who is arguing that the correct way to come to an estimate of that dense & total thing is not, again, to measure the walls of a huge city but to get down, before it is too late, on a flat thing called a map, as complete a survey as possible of all, all present ruins, small as most of them are.

They'll cry, these fat & supported characters: "Oh, they are all over the place, these, ruins!" Which is quite, quite the big & astounding fact—so much so are they all over the place that Sanchez & Co., Campeche, Mex., is not the only sand & gravel company in business: already, in this walking area from this house, I have come to learn of four sites—and of some size more than "small"—which have been already reduced to white cement in bags! (That it has taken Sanchez six years of daily grinding at the site—no where, by the way, listed as a site—the natives here in Lerma call it Casa Vieja—to take only the face off the city, may be a gauge of ((what I had no way of knowing, in Merida)) the extent of these ignored, or smiled at, spots where, 1500 years ago, for, o, say, 500 years, a people went about human business . . .

2

with a rice bowl full of the cheap rum here (35 cents by god, the qt), the kerosene lamp (my barn & hayrack), and yr long letter . . .

to start: (noting what you have noted that, the last two nights, the moon is coming to full) pick me up, thus—

by jeezus, if he didn't, having talked to me as much as no common language permits—which is a very great deal, given such a subject as, what a handsome night it was, all these houses, and the rocks below this white terraza. And the fucking night spreading itself like a peee-cock, the birdless night, not a sound but dogs, and the beginning of cocks, and the last of men along the hill back off a bit. I, lying, like Cleo or some olden knichte in stone, on the stone bed the wall of the terraza makes, the head of the stair my fine pillow. Having just thought, that fine white cayucos, would make me a fine bed for the night, its sails, for some reason, still in it, the masts, of course, shipped.

by jeezus if he didn't, having sd, bueno noche, I, bonito, he, la luna, I, magnifico, he, presto—why, I still don't know, whether, he was whistling so,—and came from the direction of the cantina, down on to the beach

anyhow, with, hasta manana, if he doesn't walk straight out into the water to that magical boat, swing himself aboard, take up his bow line, haul himself off, by the stern line, a few twenty feet (enough to take care of the fall of the tide), heave off a heavier grab-iron, start moving around fixing the sails to his liking, light himself a cigarette, and lie right down there to sleep!

jee-zus—it's handsome. I am like a kid. Tonight, swear, I never saw Venus lay down a path of light on water. She does. Has set,

now. Stars: please make me a map of the handsomer constellations (I know Orion, the two dippers (stupid names). But what
is that string of seven, or is it eight, which run down the sky to
the west of Castor & Pollux? ((All I see is the movement of the
west sky, we front the west so decisively. And the house blocks
off, the other half. But enough, what is, to make me wild, wild
(not like beautiful Lawrence, I don't mean, who, fr the full of
the moon, is sd, to have got like the throat of his fringed gen-
tians) but wild as I am which is not wild but cool, real cool

God, give me a little more of this and I shall excuse
what you say abt me, another time, my friend. For you have
said something so beautifully tonight, in this business of force:
it is (you see, I am still harping on this problem of mine, reference: constellations, Venus included (which, here, I will show
can be called KuKulCan—abandoned such, as part of THE
K's and THE PRAISES, discovering this man's death, April 5,
1208 AD, who "rose" with Venus, 8 days later, was sufficient
unto itself, so far as I was concerned) what you sd: that, force
STAYS, IS & THEREFORE STAYS, whenever, whatever:

that is what
we are concerned with

It breaks all time, & space.

muy bueno, muy

B O N I T O

3

tues.   (carlos, the letter carrier, abt due / sort of the village
idiot, i take it: walks like no fisherman, smiles like a
gringo, and is altogether not native, is "allegre," slap-
happy, and of whom I am most fond: yesterday, bring-
ing yr letter, he holds out two us air mail sts (enclosed)!
I say, how come, and, as I understood, he had noticed
that, they had not been cancelled. So he had carefully

removed them from the envelopes, and brought them
to me! So here they are, for you.

You will imagine, know-
ing my bias toward just such close use of things, how
much all these people make sense to me (coca-cola tops
are the boys' tiddley-winks; the valves of bicycle tubes,
are toy guns; bottles are used and re-used, even sold, as
cans are; old tires are the base foot-wear of this whole
peninsula (the modern Maya sandal is, rope plus Good-
year); light is candle or kerosene, and one light to a
house, even when it is a foco, for electricidad

and last night, at the store, for a beer, after they had
closed, got into one of those conversations one does, with
storekeepers, when they are sloping off: the wife was
pinching off 8 peppercorns per packet of newspaper (5
centavos) / the page was open to a television ad (Mexico
City) / they both ask me / I say MALO, MÁS MALO
QUE RADIO / but then, sez the husband, the straight
and surest question imaginable (Newsreel Companies
please note, as well as the Dept of Disappearing Culture)—POSSIBLE TO SEE LA GUERRA?

by god, that kills me: Con tells me a kid on the beach
went straight to the same, 1st question, too: possi-ble, to
see, la GUERRA? . . .

4

Sat. Feb 24   (51)

. . . Have moved ahead some on what I suppose I am here for.
And one badly damaged fresco at Chichen is a good part of
cause, joined to what I have been able to figure, from the number of ruins right back of me, & Martínez, my good fisherman
who becomes the live object to spark it all. Figure—just to keep

cutting in—to go along on this notion: that none of the characters have spotted two things (rather, they have suppressed one, and been blinded, by maize, to the other):

(1)   that the sea, precisely the FISH, was of first imaginative importance to the Maya (as well, of course, crucial to his food economy: I just might add a correlative to Sauer's beautiful shot, about maize—he made clear to the boys that the very place where starch crops can be domesticated (moderate plateaus), where maize was (the inland slopes of the cordilleras, Guatemala) cuts the people off from the most abundant source of protein and fat there is, the sea, that the earliest American farmers were just so cut off
          based on Lerma, plus some pots I have been looking over from the island of Jaina up the coast a distance, here, plus the paintings at Chichen, I take it I could, if I wanted to, demonstrate, that the movement into the Yucatan peninsula might just have been a push for protein & fats (contradicting the mystery abt same that all of these half-heads of great name keep pushing along to perpetuate their profession)

the real proof may turn out to be one of those lovely curves of live human connections. I must have sketched this bird Stromsvik, whom Con and I got drunk with, in Merida? Well, in the midst of his beer, Gus says, in Campeche, one guy, Hippolito Sánchez. The 1st day we walk into the museum here, we pick up, and take for a beer, this Sánchez (who is worrying a white puppy, with a red ribbon, that he was due to take to his girl friend, which taking I delayed a good hour, which lad Sánchez, proving himself, did the delay well by (how many do you know who can take that kind of pressing?). So this week, I saw, why, Gus, had, what had caused Gus to say, Sánchez (in fact the very same stuff which had led Gus to get this kid assigned to go to Bonampak to aid the "artists" sent there to take off copies of these newest

discovered of all Mayan frescoes): huge drawings hun-
dreds of them, of the GLYPHS on the stairway of the
major pyramid at Copan (Honduras)

my god, those you must see, some day: I am already
taking steps to see if there is not some way to get them
published. It is the only time I have found the drawings
of glyphs to begin to touch the registration of the stone
itself (and let me tell you the stones themselves are one
hell of a job to see)

this boy has the hand, eye, heart, to get them over.
And by god, if right spang in the middle of looking over
his pages do I see the most certain demonstration of the
power of the fish over these peoples I have yet oc

> Goddamn son of a bitch, if the "f" in the
machine didn't just go & bust—fuck it. Will have to go
Campeche, & hope to christ a fix possible.

Well, to hell with fish—I obviously can't say much more about
them, today, without the "f" on this fucking machine.

One other thing, tho, while it's in my head, that I wanted
to say to you: don't let even Lawrence fool you (there is nothing
in this Mexican deal, so far as "time in the sun" goes: the
way I figure it, it must have seemed attractive at a time when
the discouragement, that the machine world goes on forever,
was at its height
> but this is a culture in arrestment, which is
no culture at all (to this moment, only Sánchez gives a hint of
live taste)
> when I say that, however, I give these people much
more head, than their recent slobberers
> for the arrestment,
surely, was due to the stunning (by the Spanish) of the Indian,
400 yrs ago ((the Indian has had the toughest culture colonial-

*ism to buck of anyone, much tougher than that which Parkman
& Melville beat, 100 yrs ago, up there*

                    *culture is confidence, &
surely, Mao makes Mexico certain, ahead (Communism, here,
by the way, is solid, but is, as not in the States, nor, so far as
I have been able to judge, in Russia or Europe either, is a*
cultural *revolution, or at least the weapon of same, the only one
the Indian (like the Chinese?) has been able to get his hands
on (this whole Peninsula—where Cardenas got his familiar
name: "The Old Man," in Mayan—is a muzzle rammed for
firing)*

*The point is, the arrestment, is deceptive: it is not what fancy
outsiders have seen it as, seeking, as they were, I guess, some
alternative for themselves (like DHL & his Ladybird). Of
course, now, it is easier to kiss off the States, than, even the
30's. Yet, they should not have misled us (which is the same
as harming these Injuns: they have so fucking much future, &
no present, no present at all. (Christ, it makes me burn: their
inactivity ain't at all beautiful. They are fucking unhappy.
What graces they have are traces only, of what was & of what,
I'd guess, can be (to be a colored people today is something!
Yah?*

      *But the Negro in the States is way ahead of these 400
yr slept people! Sounds crazy? Hell, straight: yr Hyderabad
drums, for ex: jesus, the only thing you have here, any place,
when they make music (which is little) is the drum. But stacked
up against Baby Dodds or whoever, pigeon shit—or what is
most important, stacked up against these old Mayan drums I've
worked out on—five, so far, cut out of trees—you should hear
them.*

      *And the sounds they put into the feet & bottoms of
their pots, those people, to make noises, when you placed them,
or moved them, on the table! . . .*

*Point (2) above, was VIOLENCE—killing, the heart, out, etc:
those sons of bitches, those "scholars"—how they've cut that*

story out, to make the Mayan palatable to their fucking selves,
foundations, & tourists!

5

lerma   march 8

Yr letter! How it spotted itself. This way: (1) arrived precise
to eclipse of sun (½); (2) arrived at climax of long gab with
Con in which . . . I had made this proposition: that Kukulkan
vs the Chichimec was the true contest, not the Spanish, and
that I proposed to pick up again, now here, on the life of this
very great man, saying to Con, that, with so much registration
of him in codices, frescoes, stone cutting, stucco, it should be
as possible, or more, to recreate him as, that Barlow, from mss.,
sought to do same by Montezuma:

                                    had just sd, "I forgot to
tell you, that, at Champoton, after you took the bus last Sunday, I got into conversation with a bar boy, there, and, talking
abt the Isla Cuyo (the remnant now standing in the sea of the
pyramid K had erected for himself, there, on departing Tula-
ward, he having done his work, here), it was my notion, that,
that he had the imagination to build *in the sea*, was another
sign of how unique he was" (asking myself, the relation of
same act to (1) the fact that the Maya hereabouts put their
cities (in contrast to all since) on the hill over the sea ("Señor
gusta monte," sd the lady, fr whom, bananas, on the road in,
one day), (2) the Island of Jaina, just above us here, abt as far
north of us as Champoton is south, and not yet visited because
it *has* to be *reached by sea* (had most beautiful workmen in
clay), and (3) that, on the east coast, the big beautiful place
is TULUM, and, the *Island* of Cozumel (by map in yesterday
fr Tulane, the sites on Cozumel are thick ((propose to go there,
if possible to swing it: three days by sailing vessel· from
Progreso))

when LETTER-LIGHT, comes in the midst of a context unduplicatable—(1) the stir outside with all, *all*, kids & grown ups, watching, the eclipsa, excited (contrast to States, abt 1930, when, a total eclipse, and only me and the birds, apparently, aware, until it was suddenly dark) here, with no real shrinkage of light, yet, everyone, these descendants of astronomers, than whom none more effective than one Kukulkan, apparently ((the month CEH, as, I believe, in last letter I identified as HIS new fire ceremony—Spinden dates its institution as 1168 with a Day 1 Knife, when K started a year count as Year 1 Knife, and in Year 2 Reed, 1194-5, he declared the Fire Ceremony to be celebrated at intervals of 52 years)) all of them, with smoked glass and old film and rolled up newspapers, anything, looking, upward; (2) the conversation, me still beating around, these things

&

(3) CARLOS WALKS IN WITH YR NEWS, YR NEWS, BRO, OF K & a sea-horse (for same thing, a sea-horse, is also precise: using as fetish to hold down yr letters in the wind which sweeps through this room, what do I have, have had since third day after arrival, as present from a boy I have never seen since? and same thing I have thought again & again, it's light, and I should like to send it to you & Ann & kids as SIGN, but haven't because, to box something seems beyond huge, for to get a letter off, a money order say, is already proved murder: one for book fr Merida lost already!

And now it is too late. For you have it, already. And have made me the present! Beautiful. And tell Slater, for me, he's HOT. Or so I'd guess, round abt now, with, what is in hand:

Let me go back.

I: why I still beat up against this biz of, getting rid of nomination, so that historical material is free for forms now, is

Ez's epic solves problem by his ego: his single emotion breaks all down to his equals or inferiors (so far as I

can see only two, possibly, are admitted, by him, to be
his betters—Confucius, & Dante. Which assumption,
that there are intelligent men whom he can outtalk, is
beautiful because it destroys historical time, and

thus creates the methodology of the Cantos, viz, a space-
field where, by inversion, though the material is all time
material, he has driven through it so sharply by the
beak of his ego, that, he has turned time into what we
must now have, space & its live air

((secondary contrast is Joyce, who, it comes to me
now, did not improve on Duns Scotus Erigenus, or
the Irish of the time the Irish were the culture-bosses,
what was it, 7th–9th century, or something: he tried
to get at the problem by running one language into
another so as to create a universal language of the
unconscious. Which is, finally, mush & shit, that is,
now. Not so, then, DSE or Irishers, for then Europe
was, both in language & dream, of that order.

(((further thot: Joyce, the Commercial Traveller:
the worship of IARichards—by the same people, accurately enough, who mug Joyce—is
more honest: that is, that this international-
izing of language is more relevant to commerce,
now, than it is to the aesthetic problem.
((((all this a bet-
ter way to say, he, ENDER)

the primary contrast, for our purposes is, BILL: his Pat
is exact opposite of Ez's, that is, Bill HAS an emotional
system which is capable of extensions & comprehensions
the ego-system (the Old Deal, Ez as Cento Man, here
dates) is not. Yet

by making his substance historical of one city (the Joyce
deal), Bill completely licks himself, lets time roll him

under as Ez does not, and thus, so far as what is the more important, methodology, contributes nothing, in fact, delays, deters, and hampers, by not having busted through the very problem which Ez has so brilliantly faced, & beat

Which ought to—if my mouth had words in it, this morning—bring you to see why I hammer, on, nomination, thus:

each of the above jobs are HALVES, that is, I take it (1) that the EGO AS BEAK is bent and busted but   (2) whatever it is that we can call its replacement (Bill very much a little of it) HAS, SO FAR, not been able to bring any time so abreast of us that we are in this present air, going straight out, of our selves, into it

You see, I followed you, a bit back, when, in responding on Tarot & Maya, you sd, sure, & it's whatever you or anyone makes hot, is hot. Of course.

& two: that, we already have both (1) the ego as responsible to more than itself and (2) absolute clarity, that, time, is done, as effect of work in hand

Perhaps, as I sd before, I am only arguing with myself, that is, I am trying to see how to throw the materials I am interested in so that they take, with all impact of a correct methodology AND WITH THE ALTERNATIVE TO THE EGO-POSITION

I keep thinking, it comes to this: culture displacing the state. Which is my guess as to why Ez sounds so flat, when, he is just talking, when, he is outside the Cantos, say, that walker of his, than which there is, yet, no better
(so much of Ez is, the 19th century stance:
PROTEST, (Dahlberg is the funny man, of same biz:
they both wld love to have been, who was it,
Lousie 14th, "l'état, c'est moi"?

what burns me, is, they never speak, in their
slash at the State or the Economy, basically,
for anyone but themselves. And thus, it is
Bohemianism

and much too late, just abt as late as before
Fourier, Marx, & Nietzsche, not to mention
the real guys, then, Riemann or any of the
geometers who were really cutting ahead

Tho, again, here, one has to give Ez his due: that he did
write KULCH

Which ought to get us to II, or, Kulkulkan. This way:

why
the problem is tougher than Ez's throw, or Bill's failure, is
that, the shift is SUBSTANTIVE (it delights me, to recognize, that, the word has that other meaning, of "noun"!)

that
is, another reason why i don't think Ez's toucan works after
1917 is, that, after that date, the materials of history which
he has found useful are not at all of use (nor are Bill's, despite
the more apparent homogeneity: date 1917, not only did Yurrup
(West, Cento, Renaissance) go, but such blueberry America as
Bill presents (Jersey dump-smoke covering same) also WENT
(that is, Bill, with all respect, don't know fr nothing abt what
a city *is*)

the which says this: that the substances of history
now useful lie outside, under, right here, anywhere but in the
direct continuum of society as we have had it (of the State,
same, of the Economy, same, of the Politicks: Ez is traitor as
Dante was, to Florence: the difference of F to USA is not difference at all, other than, the passage of time & time's dreary
accumulations by repetition

(((something of this must have
been what Razl meant, when
he sd, HISTORY IS UNI-
VERSAL MONOTONY)))

(*Note:* I note that I assume history is prime, even now. I assume it is. I assume this one thing—man's curiosity abt what his brother zopalotes have been about—comes through to us straight from that previous civilization, and is the one thread we better damn well hang on to. And the only one.

Perhaps because it is as much prime, as, an eclipse?

The substance has changed. Period. BUT: we are confronted, as men forever are, by the LAG. Our fellow cits are, I take it, quite easily thrown off by any noun which contains Z's and X's. (Not, again, that, thus superficially, it matters a good god damn: bust them over the heads. Right. Only, what i am saying is, that, to use X's and Z's makes for the difficulties John Adams, or Kung Fu Sze, or even Omeros, don't. ((Or is this just a little bit argumentative, & petulant, as one is, when the work is not done, and one is talking abt it instead.))
((Doesn't matter. For, as you'd guess, the operation is otherwise, is, actually, the other edge: how *was* this Kukulkan, how are you, Mister C)))

How can I pick up these injuns—that is, as Stephens, Prescott, Parkman did not so pick them up 100 yr agone, that, at the same moment of time as one H. Melville, they made them stick as he did, Pacifica? What's wrong—or, likewise, Sumeria. Or mao. Or usa, today.

NO. Erase the above. Somewhere I've been dragged off the methodological, here, by my own mention of the substantive. And am sucked into a substantive argument. Which is not what we're here for. Let me try it another way. For it's still this man Kukulkan we are talking abt.

Shots:

> (1) are not the Maya the most important characters
> in the whole panorama (diorama was the word
> contemporary to above fine 4 workers) simply be-
> cause the TOP CLASS in their society, the bosses,
> were a class whose daily business was KNOWL-
> EDGE, & its OFF-SHOOT, culture?
>
>> that thus a man of K's temper &
>> interest could become Big Boss, &
>> then, God?
>
>> and that any such society
> goes down easily before a gun? or bows & arrows,
> when Chichemecs come along with same? ((The
> absolute quote here, is, one prime devil, Goeb-
> bels, who sd: "When I hear the word 'kultur' I
> reach for my gun."))
>
> (2) that such a society is precisely the contrary (really
> the contrary, not the opposite, to use Blake's care-
> ful discrimination, and, by so doing, show up the
> collective or communist deal for what it is, and
> will continue to be as long as the rest of the world
> wants what America has had

Comes up, out out of the sea, a sea
horse (my question is, where
here
do the rains
come from, is the serpent
who shall fight the jaguar
another norther, of
another season, is
weather, here, as on the earth because
the earth turns eastward, is
all movements, as was the people's coming, is it from
the west?

they say
he was the wind, they say
also rain, anyway
he was water, not
sun fire not this heat which makes the day less
than the night

he wore a hat, a sort of silly hat, had
short breeches, a tortoise back with mirror on it, and
a tail: he died
just as the heat was at its worst, just
on the day the fields were burnt, just that day the morning
star rose anew
             his eyes, she sd,
             were like a caracol. And when he left us, he
             walked straight out into the sea, west
                         he was also
                         a bachelor
                                   but what
seemed most important, he
was just, was
a child
of water, they figured it, was
precisely what
they needed, was
the image of
(Well! To hell with that. Pardon me. Get up off my
face, olson.)
themselves.

It is a beautiful thing, what Slater found. You are right, of
course: it bears right in on what I have been turning over. I
figure, now, that why (as I think I told you) I abandoned him in
the two throws of The K's and The P's, was, that, it is this thing,
of the sea, which one finds out here. And nobody told me. And
which sea is the addition to him as Venus, which, makes up a
package.

A *favor*: if you have an encyclopedia at hand, or any source, could you write me what this damned star Venus does with itself in a year? That is, is there a coincidence of its brightest brightness with April 12th or thereabouts? We await, e.g., that day, or c., because, they tell us, on that date the farmers burn their fields, and, for a month, it is here as tho there were an eclipse—or as it was, there, last fall, when the Canadian woods were burning down   FORGET IT. I guess the time has come for me to dig this biz. And it's large. And better be done whole (all I was after I'll tell you another day. But 1st:

What cools me, is a sentence like this fr Spinden:

"Date I: 11- 8-14- 3-16, 10 Cib 4 Yax, May 5, 1136

This phenomenon took place before the Toltecs had conquered Chichen Itza but easily enough it may represent data upon which Quetzalcoatl worked and which possibly he presented in his Sacred Book."

or

"In the Vienna Codex the Venus staff" which Quetz is chief bearer of "is stuck in a valley between two hills beside a trumpet shell" (which trumpet shell Con & I find plenty of—even found one at K's Isla—and is, of course, our sea-shell, or, here, the CARACOL (the astronomers' house at Chichen, is, a snail!)

It's the damndest thing, what a cat I got by the tail. For, you see, here is this supposed land-maize people who use
(1) for the house which brought them culture, the astronomy house, a SEA-SHELL
(2) for the man who appears to have made the language of this people for time in the universe available to all neighboring peoples, a SEA-HORSE!

And—this had broke in on me before I got yr letter with Slater's shot, yesterday—THE EVIDENCES Spinden here

88

above is referring to, are not Maya, but MIXTEC, in other words, of the Central Valley of Mexico, not Yucatan. SO THAT, the whole picture has shifted wider & out, west: in fact, what i ought to be, am, proposing, is, THE SEA IN MAYA & MEXICAN CULTURES & ECONOMIES.

AND
AND, somewhere in this mixing of the two geographies is the key to why there is a KUKULKAN here, & QUETZ there: same man, same imagery (the serpent with fuzz) (SEA-SERPENT?)

What the astronomy establishes, is, that the complex is WATER: that is, Venus-sign (Q & K Venus-God, April 13, 1208 thereafter) is "Nine WIND." Is also RAIN (the seasonal need). Is also; somehow, SERPENT (contrary of sun, which is, Jaguar). Is—shall we allow, for the present—SEA-H. In other words, see what I mean: snails, for noise, water, for maize, and a man, fr the west, where (does it) the wind (yes, northers) & the rain (also?) come from . . .

(O, yes, as of the wind: the drawing of K or Q most like ann's s . . h . . . . , is, actually, not of him himself but of the wind, God K of the Codices, who is, to be sure, by reasoning from a like union in Mexican mythology, seen as K:

let me send back that drawing, for, Ann's to me:

sat march 17

christamiexcited. getting that load off my heart, to you, thursday, did a trick. for i pulled out, that afternoon, down the road
AND BROKE THRU—

> hit a real spot, which had spotted fr bus,
> and which same, apparently, untouched:
> Con & I came back with bags of sherds
> & little heads & feet—all lovely things
>
> then, yesterday, alone, hit further south,
> and smash, dug out my 1st hieroglyphic
> stone! plus two possible stela (tho, no
> crowbar, so no proof)
>
> and today I went to hit again, while the
> run's on: and the joy that everything I
> can get to, in an hour (necessary, however, to risk getting a ride back, bumming: last night, took until 10:30, with
> Con, here, sure, fr a conversation of warning fr a friend the night before, scaring
> the shit out of both of us, that snakes will
> get you! she saw me in the wilds with no
> one to suck the wound, and this morning,
> the zopalotes eating me, with the rising
> sun!) To tell the truth, I was scared,
> yesterday, where I was, for the 1st half
> hour. Then, the excitement, the loveliness, the hell with it . . .

Had started to reply . . . But my nerves are so bunched toward
these ruins, I better go and get back to these things later, if you
will understand, please. For I am wild for it.

Example: the big baby I spotted yesterday means CHUNCAN means TRUNK OF THE SKY—and by god, the pyramid is so sharp and high it is just that, and most beautiful, high over the sea and the land (more like a watch-tower than anything templish . . .

7

tuesday, march 20

. . . picking up, going back, over: (1) Ann, was shooting good, on the agronomy . . . only it's a little different, and, another measure of—a damn good measure of—what machines, in their laziness, lead to: viz—unlike India, the soil, here, is most shallow, a few inches, & only occasionally, in drift pockets, 6 inches or more. So the struggle of the roots is intense. But a long time ago the boys beat it this way. It's grass that is the big enemy of maize, the only real one, for they burn off the bush, before they plant. But grass keeps coming in. And in the old days, they were able to stand it off—for as long as seven years (the maximum life of a milpa)—by weeding out the grass by *hand*. But then came the machete. And with it, the victory of grass in *two* years. For ever since that iron, the natives cut the grass, and thus, without having thought about it, spread the weed-seed, so that the whole milpa is choked, quickly choked, and gone, forever, for use for, maize (grass is so tough it doesn't even let bush or forest grow again!)

One curious corollary, that, the Communist future of this peninsula will have to reckon with: that, the ground is such, and its topography so humped & rocked, that, still, the ancient method of planting—with a pointed stick, and sowing, with the hands—is far superior to any tractor or planter or whatever.

So I wonder very much about Slater's pass, that the Maya were far too intelligent a race to exhaust their soil, not to speak, as you are right to question, of his observation, that they were a highly spiritual race and such races always regard their soil as sacred:

for example, what i can't find anything out about, is WATER. Judging from the bizness here now—and adding it to the *apparent* fact that the Maya depended, for water, upon these accidents of nature, where the upper limestone crust collapsed, and created these huge cenotes, near which they built their cities—I'd guess that this people had a very ancient way of *not improving on nature*, that is, that it is not a question of either intelligence or spirituality, but another thing, something Americans have a hard time getting their minds around, a form or bias of attention which does not include *improvements*

AND (by that law of the toilet, beds, etc., I wrote you about once, from Washington—how I can never worry) I'm not one myself to say they were *backward*, *are* backward (my god, talk about the stars here: I ought to get off to you about the *flesh* here! Jesus, to ride a bus with these people, of a Sunday, down the coast, the stopping, the variation of quality between, say, Seybaplaya (allegre) and La Jolla (a sugar cane plant there, and a bottom, all, creatures, most of them, garage proletariat—to steal, an accurate, phrase)

BUT, the way the bulk of them still (the "unimproved") wear their flesh! It is something I never had the occasion to guess, except in small pieces, isolated moments like, say, an Eyetalian family, or some splinter, not making itself clear enough to take over my assurances. For this is very much the result, I'd take it, as, the agriculture, the water problem: the flesh is worn as a daily thing, like the sun, is—& only in this sense—a common, carried as the other things are, for use. And not at all exclusively sexual, as, it strikes me, the flesh is hardened, and like wires, focused ("foco" is the name for an electric light bulb, here) in the industrial States. The result (and this is what I think is actually the way to put what Slater makes spiritual or sacred) is, that the individual peering out from that flesh is precisely himself, is, a curious wandering animal (it is so very beautiful, how animal the eyes are, when the flesh is not worn so close it chokes, how human and individuated the look comes out: jeesus, when you are rocked, by the roads, against any of them —kids, women, men—it's so very gentle, so granted, the feel, of touch—none of that pull, away, which, in the States caused me, for so many years, the deepest sort of questions about my own structure, the complex of my own organism, I felt so very much this admission these people now give me

This is not easy to state, I guess. BUT OF EXTREME IMPORTANCE. For I come on, here, what seems to me the real, live clue to the results of what I keep gabbing about, *another* humanism. For it is so much a matter of resistance—like I tried to say, about, *leaving* the difficulties, not removing them, by *buying* the improvements so readily available at the corner. You buy something all right, but what gets forgotten is, that you sell, in that moment of buying—you sell a whole disposition of self which very soon plunders you just where you are not looking. Or so, it seems.

The trouble is, with this imagery, of industrial man. I distrust it, as (1) too easy (2) too modern and (3) too much, not contrary, but merely oppositional. For the shift, which took away, (is taking away, so rapidly, that I shall soon not be able to get into Campeche, it is such an ugly ("feo," is their word) demonstration of what happens when COMMERCE comes in) —how do you get at what happened? when did some contrary principle of man get in business? why? what urge

well, that's not hard, I know—i figure it always was, only, once (or still, here, at Seybaplaya—and a bit back, Lerma, before electricity) these big-eared, small-eyed, scared-flesh characters stayed as the minority, were not let out of, their holes. Because there was a concept at work, not surely "sacred," just a disposition to keep the attention poised in such a way that there was time to (1) be interested in expression & gesture of all creatures including at least three large planets enough to create a system of record which we now call hieroglyphs; (2) to mass stone with sufficient proportion to decorate a near hill and turn it into a firetower, or an observatory, or as one post of an enclosure in which people, favored by its shadows, might swap camotes for shoes; (3) to fire clay, not just to sift and thus make cool water, or, to stew iguana, or fish, but to fire it so that its handsomeness put ceremony where it also belongs, in the most elementary human acts. And when a people are so disposed, it should come as no surprise that, long before any of these accomplishments, the same people did an improvement, if one likes, of nature—the domestication of maize—which is still talked of as one of the world's wonders!

It is all such a delicate juggling of weights, this culture business —exactly like, I'd guess, what is the juggling of any one of us with the given insides. Which is why generalization is, a greased slide.

Christ, these hieroglyphs. Here is the most abstract and formal deal of all the things this people dealt out—and yet, to my taste, it is precisely as intimate as verse is. Is, in fact, verse. Is their verse. And comes into existence, obeys the same laws that, the coming into existence, the persisting of verse, does.

Which leads me to use again Ruth Benedict's excellent proposition (to counter the notion that, the Maya, having done so much, need also have developed an agronomy which would not have exhausted their soil and a system of rain-gathering which would also have licked the thirst problem): says Benedict,

. . . techniques of cultural change which are limited
only by the *unimaginativeness of the human mind*

Or which, perhaps, is just a little bit the bitterness of an old-maid almost-Communist before she died. It seems to me now, she over-loads, by using "imagination," even negatively—a little bit too much modern Hamletism (I am thinking of Hamlet to Horatio (is it) on what a glory man is, the top creature, what nature, was working toward, etc.) Benedict is still the reverse of same. One needs to be quieter—but still not miss the point: that, in a given lifetime a man, or, in a given expression, a culture cannot get any more done than it can get done: that time, & our life-machine, are not infinitely extensible. Which dream—the Renaissance, & all ecstatic propositions—is well dead. We'll know more and do more if the limits—there'll be more reaches, etc.

My point is, what more do we have the privilege to ask of the Maya than same Maya offered . . .

CHUN-CAN, by the way, which I told you was TRUNK OF THE SKY, is—says Martínez—not that (which is what the Seybanos told me) but TRUNK OF THE SERPENT. He says, to be the 1st, it would have to be CHUN-CAAN. (Which of course it may have been.)

8

Lerma   March 22   51

It is Holy Week in this Spanish nation, so I imagine the reason we have not had any mail since the weekend is, that the airplanes are blessing themselves, and doing other services over the middle of the Gulf. It irritates me, as do all Sundays, holidays and such: tho yesterday, I shall say it was pleasant, sitting in a Coney Island stand (the best cafe Campeche can offer, on a sidewalk—o, for Vera Cruz, on such a day), eating turkey tacos, & drinking mineral water! (We had had to go in, at 10 A.M. to settle an argument over the rent of this house—which we lost, I am afraid: the two owners got into a snarl a month ago, and I was hoping we could take advantage of it to force the rent back to what we expected to pay when we came.

But I guess not: it was fun, trying—and much worth while, for 5 bucks difference, here, is a good week's food.

In any case, the whole uproar brings on the problems of what I ought to do, running out, as I am, so fast, of funds. It burns my arse, to be put to it—and just when I begin to pick up, feel freshened, toughened, and hoisted forward. It is that old problem, how a man, whose goods are not bought, whose daily drive turns out to be non-economic (Corman tells me we are all dollar-an-issue men) eats, sleeps, gets on, with his work.

I keep turning over, where to strike out, for a stake . . . The only hitch is, the extremity fast approaches, god damn it. Which interrupts my mind. And deters, deters!!

But not much. Have been digging the old Maya chronicles, the last couple of days, and come up with interesting stuff on Quetz-Kukul—and the question of, sea origins. Will be folding it yr-way, I suspect, soon. One curious thing is, that the place of origin (in the legends) keeps coming up as TULE (also Tula, Tullan, Tulapan). And it is sd to be the place where he, "the great father-priest," was,—where, in fact, according to a Quiche-Maya tale, he gave the first captain who set out for Guatemala-Yucatan, a present called "*Giron Gagal.*" (What in christ that is, nobody knows.) One other curious thing about these chronicles, is, the "Persian" look to so many of them. (I got on to this slant, sometime ago, when I found rewriting GATE & C, that water in Sumerian is "a," & in Maya, "ha.")

But this TULE is curious in other ways (not to mention the fact that, in one people's version it is on the other side of the ocean to the east, & in another, to the west): the wildest of all, is, what you will remember, that *ultima Thule*, was the outermost reach of the world to the ancients, was, to the Greeks, Thoule, or Thyle. In the light of Waddell, I should like to know (or Berard, as well as Waddell, for that matter) if that word goes back behind the Greeks to the Phoenicians, Cretans, Sumerians.

I say this, for another reason—which goes very deep into the whole question these Maya raise (and it's treacherous ground, where all that I have seen try to walk on it, have fallen for the most dangerous Nordicism there is). But it is this evidence (you see it all around you here, and clearly not from Spanish mixture) that there was an Armenoid-Caucasian physical type just as clearly as there was a Mongoloid type among the ancient Maya. (Hippolito, for ex., was telling Con and me—with considerable excitement—about a Lacandon Indian who was his & Stromsvik's guide when they were at Bonampak three yrs ago (these Lacandones are an isolated tribe in Chiapas, near the Guatemala border, who have stayed in a state of arrestment apparently equal to the period of the Maya *before* the cultivation of maize—which goes back, maybe, 3 millennia before Christ, or, into that area of time which coincides with the opening out of the Persian and Mediterranean world by the Sumerians.) Hippolito was struck by this man's whiteness, his scimitar of a nose, and the whole caucasianism of his mind and behavior.

The funny thing is, I have come on one Maya "expert" who is pushing an argument—strangely enough—which is most close to Waddell's (tho this bird Jakeman obviously doesn't know Waddell at all). It is this: that the Itzas (who, he declares, were the priest-tribe of the Maya, the inventors of glyphs, astronomy, & the building) were the Caucasians, and can be distinguished precisely from the Mongoloids, who were the subject people, the farmers, the workers, etc. And of course his most telling argument (though he does not use it—though maybe he does: not sure yet) is that business of Quetzal-Kukul, as *white*, *bearded*, and from beyond the eastern sea.

Of course I balk at same, or at least resist, simply because I take it, racism has to be kept at the end of a stick. Or put it this way: until we have completely cleaned ourselves of the biases of westernism, of greekism, until we have squared away at historical time in such a manner that we are able to see

Sumer as a point from which *all* "races" (speaking of them culturally, not, biologically) egressed, we do not have permission to weight the scale one way or another (for example, Jakeman, leaves, so far as I have read him, the invention of maize to the Mongoloids, as well as the arts of ceramics, weaving, and baskets! And, *contra* (contra all these prejudiced Nordics, among whom I include Hooton, who has sd, from skull-measurements, that it is true, there were Caucasians here), there remains China, ancient and modern China. Until the lads can verify that the Chinese, as well as the people of India, came off from the Tigris-Euphrates complex, they better lie low with their jumps to conclude that only the Caucasian type was the civilizing type of man). ((As you know, this whole modern intellectual demarche, has, at its roots, a negative impulse, deeper, even, than the anti-Asia colonialism of Europe: at root, the search is, to unload, to disburden themselves, of Judaism, of Semitism.))

What excites me, is, a whole series of scholarly deductions which widen out the rear of the Maya sufficiently for me to pick up confirmations to my imaginative thesis of the sea, that is, of migration. (I had much joy this morning showing Martínez how the peoples of the Pacific made maps—I was using match-sticks to stand for those extraordinary charts of sticks and twine by which the Polynesians & others made the voyages from the Malay Peninsula out across that space. And trying, in this still struggling Spanish—"practico," as they tell me, I still resist studying books of same—to describe to him those huge out-riggers the Pacific peoples used!) . . .

9

thursday   march 15

crazy, not to have written you. not doing a hell of a lot: not well, either of us, or, for that matter much of anyone around Lerma—peculiar weather, either too hot or, the last three days a wild and beautiful norther, the wind blowing the hell out of a new moon. One day, the 1st, it was like any small Maine fishing village in storm: not even the muchachas out in the streets, every house barred, and severe, and if a man about, wrapped (like pictures of Mexicans) to his teeth in his cotton blanket (no such handsome things as serapes here, just cheap cotton blankets—& the choicest hat is a fucking chauffeur's cap!)

   i can't quite figure, what's wrong with me, but never knew a better law than, if the body lags, it's somewhere else the lag is. Figure it's a huge shell-hole i'm in, from recent firing. And me just lying there, figuring, where i was hit, or, better, what bore & raise of gun got me.

   Anyhow, nothing raises me. And I waste time reading, murders (which all seem written by those filthies, newspapermen). (((A library of 'em, here, fr the wreck of a shrimper, American, beached on the farm of San Lorenzo, 10 kms down the road. Never read em before, much.)))

Went off by myself, the grey day, down the rd to sd farm, just for the motion. And by god picked myself off another ruin: right the hell on top of a little mt right the hell up over the sea! These Maya shure went for vistas . . .

But it's hieroglyphs, which are the real pay-off, the inside stuff, for me. And that's not in situ, that is, you can't see them—why Sánchez is so very much the value, for me, here (he came to dinner Monday night, and by god if he doesn't come in with the whole set of little books published in Campeche with his drawings of same, damndest sweetest present, and, too much, as you'd say, too much . . .

What wilds me, is, that here, in these things, is the intimate art (as against the mass & space of the buildings (god-stuff), and the corn-god, woman-temple, sacrifice-stone (the social purpose))

   Or Jaina! Jesus, what work, there: the only trouble is, they know, and it's guarded, & for me to dig, no go: have to be an official, have to be what I was talking about, above: just one

99

thing, in Museo, Campeche, two clay things, abt a hand's span tall, of the calix of a flower with a human being rising, right where the pistil would be! Incredible delicacy, & sureness: as in the glyphs, only, the glyphs already one stage formal, one stage set: the same glyphs, with variations, fr north to south! (What a bunch of live, working men, in this business, there were, wherever, there was a site: ex., down the road, Sunday before last, a place called Pueblo Nuevo, the site no more than 75 feet over-all, and spang, there still, a stone-glyph!) . . .

Still going along on Venus, or, as they called her, *Noh ek* (the great star) or, *xux ek* (the wasp star—which sounds, this way: shoosh ek)

& the story seems to be, her attraction, beside her brightness, there for all to see, is: she's the asymmetrical one, of the Big Three, she's the one who is off the count, and does not put in regular appearance: works on a round of 584 days, but, is a real witch, in that she is two, that is, for eight months is morning star, then disappears completely for three months, to reappear as evening star for eight months, after which time she takes a dive for 14 days, to begin again, to be born, out of the eastern sea, from the balls of, her father, the sun

I like her, and like that they called her—why—the wasp, why . . .

10

monday, mars (Or, as I figure it comes out, on the Maya
calendar: CEH, day AKBAL
(Ceh meaning the New Fire Ceremony, Insti-
tuted by Kukulkan, 1159 AD or c.

. . . yesterday was a bitch, & beautiful: we took 7 A.M. bus down coast, to a glyph, then set off up the road back, walking some 8 kilometres to a place on coast called Sihoplaya, which same beach is only equalled by Oregon coast: we stripped, and washed each other with the sand (not sand, but minute fragments of shells) and crawled around that whiteness and green, out into a submarine garden.

But the sun is already beyond taking, at midday, and of course, like mad dogs, we get caught out: we ended, under a small bridge over the only tidal river between here & the next large town, Chapoton. At which place the bus caught me in as I was born, in, that thing which is like beginning, for me (tagged by the Annisquam), a tidal, same! So much slugged today, too much to rise to, in the mails, (1) Tozzer's Maya Grammar (by air mail thru Corman) and (2) MAP of sites hereabout fr Tulane. So I write you, to cheer me up! And for the hell of it, let me send you a leetla thing, for the throw, for what it is, notes, for a beginning

        The fish is speech. Or see
        what, cut
        in stone
        starts. For

        when the sea breaks, watch
        watch, it is the
        tongue, and

        he who introduces the words (the
        interlocutor), the
        beginner of the word, he

        you will find, he
        has scales, he
        gives off motion as

        in the sun the wind the light, the fish
        moves

lerma march 27

Over the house, last night, 3 A.M., the SOUTHERN CROSS!
please tell Slater that, & that, with a flashlight, I confirmed
it with, his map: tell him, the SC, here, is, at that hour, much
like, & a gentler, say, feminine counterpart to, earlier, in the
west, ORION: tell him, another thanks, for his drawings &
note, on the SeaHorse (which came in yesterday, along with yr
other testimonial)

tell him this: that, it is quite quite true, that, here, the life of a
night sky is very thick & close—and that same fact i have not
seen anywhere admitted as good & sufficient reason for the Maya
exploitation of same, that, in fact, in contrast to the day, which
is so goddamn strong it is whited out, is, so pervasive as to
make it necessary that one either blind oneself to it or hide, the
night is delicious, & the sky so swift in the passage of the
constellations, in the play of their colors, that it is impossible to
leave

(one good & sufficient reason why there was, here, a
class of men who mastered this other life is, I just bet, that, if
you could choose, if you did not have to work fields, or whatever, by the light of, the sun, then, by god, you'd do what I've
always sd any civilized man wld do, arrange it, that, you lived in
the night not, the day!)

sure, the Mayans, too, hid from THE
WASP, as they called her, that STAR: she gives you the jim-
mies right now, the other night, settling down in the west, and
throwing such a fit of light & color, you'd swear she was going
to blow right up in yr face then & there SHOOSH ECK

at which point i transfer to you how the Maya took it the other
two citizens behaved:

moon is girl, living with grandfather, weaving. sun is not yet
sun, is a young man full of himself, who wants this girl, &
poses as great hunter, to win her first looking. to come closer
he borrows the nature of hummingbird, but, while drinking
honey out of the tobacco flowers near her house, grandpa pings
him with a clay shot fr blowgun. moon picks sun-bird to bosom,
then to room, then sun to consciousness, then sun to human
shape, and business! he persuades her to elope. but g-pop gets
rain to toss bolts at pair fleeing in canoe: sun converts to turtle
and escapes, but moon, trying on crab shell, is not protected
enough & is killed.

dragonflies collect moon's flesh & blood in 13 hollow logs. after
13 days sun uncovers logs, finds 1st 12 to contain all known
noxious insects & snakes, which, released, spread all over the
world. log 13 reveals moon, restored, to life

only moon has no cunt, ah. deer, however, remedies same
defect, & sun & moon do it, the first persons to have such
pleasure ((some passage of time))

enter sun's older brother, creating triangle of sky, for elder
bro. is venus, who comes to live with sun & moon. sun begins to
suspect there is something going on between moon & big star,
they are so much together. by a trick he exposes them, & moon,
dispirited, is sitting alone by riverwater when a vulture persuades her to go with him to the house of king vulture. Which
she does, becoming his wife.

sun (the dope) seeking her, borrows skin of a small deer, hides
under it, & when vultures come to eat what they think is the
carcass of same, sun snatches one, gets on his back, & rides off
to king vulture's house, where he recovers moon, who is somewhat reluctant to return

at which stage, for reasons of cause or not, sun & moon go up
into the sky to assume their celestial duties. but sun finds there

is one last thing he must do to this dame before all's right with the orb: the people on earth complain that because moon is so goddamned bright they can't sleep & it is always the same as day. so sun, to dim his dame's brightness, knocks out one of her eyes

the tale has this superior gimmick, for its ending: eclipses, sd the old ones, were nothing more nor less than fights between sun & moon, presumably because sun can't forget moon's promiscuity, though the Quiche have it that moon, anyway, is erratic, very much a liar (is constantly telling sun tales about the way the people on the earth misbehave, drink too much, etc.), and as difficult to understand as any bitch is.

I'mp tellink you, Robert, yure right, i got a horn by its tail! and fr the way it looks today (i mean precisely today, things keep shifting so as i cut away at my ignorance), that introductory glyph (of the fish) which led me in, was sign of where i am intended to go:
                    and i sure back off! for it is straight forward into GLYPHS (like you probably smelled, the last few communications). and that's one pisser of a task (& the bitch of it is, is no way to raise dough to continue here, any smart guy saying, such study is years, & in lieu of any immediate addition to "knowledge," how can you justify staying there, instead of here, to make the same study?
                    which, of course, is cockeyed, for, it is by being here where that life was that i pick up on same, including glyphs, and would best continue, but (again) who knows that but thee & who:
                    it is a joker, straight: this way, that, these Maya are worth remembering because they were hot for the world they lived in & hot to get it down by way of a language which is loaded to the gills of the FIRST GLYPH with that kind of imagination which the kerekters have a way of calling creative

yet i have yet to find *one* man among all who have worked this street in the last century who is, himself, confident of his taste, is even possessed of that kind of taste, or drive towards a hot world, which is called creative power!

and the result, of course, is, that the discrepancy between what the maya did and what these birds are finding out about it is just another of those gaps which confirm the old man in his shot, that, it was not original sin, good bro. possum, which was the fall of man, but o-riginal, in-nate, stupidity!

ex., glyphs: give you or me the "alphabet," just the rudiments of the first meanings, plus a Maya dictionary and as full a knowledge as possible of tales (such as the above), and by god if we wouldn't walk all over them as to what the rest of the story is! i swear (adding as long a time as possible just being here to observe, not so much contemporary maya (another of the wise boys' phoney smartnesses) but the *geography* in which the old maya lived.

excuse me, there's no use beating you with sticks i ought to be getting the chance to beat some others with. and anyway, what i want to get to, with you, is, at the nature of this *language,* of which the glyphs are the most beautiful expression (much more beautiful, by the way, than the codices, which are late & Mexican (pictographic, not, as were the Maya, both ideographic & phonetic) and much more beautiful (due to the limits of stone plus the limits of language) than the sculpture or, for that matter, the architecture . . .

lerma   wednesday   march 28

. . . don't let ann think, she, & los animales, marine especially,
are being left behind. for all this started fr a fish (the INTRO-
DUCTORY GLYPH), and it will come flying home, fins & all:
yesterday, for example, I found further evidence (& right spang
out of Sánchez's drawings) that the big boy of it all (J. Eric S.
Thompson) must be wrong, when he sees the fish as a rebus of a
mythological monster more like a crocodile than an actual fish
(the land-bias, of the mayistas).

> Ex.: "The fish and the Imix prefix to this god's
> glyph (God L, Dresden, p. 46) are probably
> clues to his identification (he wears fish in
> his headdress twice), ((Imix, sez T, is water-
> lily)), for both symbols are primarily those
> of the earth crocodile, and secondary attri-
> butes of all deities of the soil and the under-
> world."

It is as underworld figure, or passenger, that T sees Quetzal-
Kukan, throughout his book: that is, he is both Venus & the
sun because they go down into the underworld. And so fish,
water-lilies, & conch shell, because, by way of ponds, I guess,
plus geologic deposits in the limestone, perhaps!, associated
with his disappearance, &, reappearance! (come here, leo, fro,
benius!)

And you can tell Slater that Thompson hasn't even guessed at
sea-horse! (He's a respectable worker, this T, but, I very much
surmise he's playing with things he ain't bought the rights to.
But it will take us a little time to find out!)

As a fact the beauty of Copan is, one small beauty is that it is
precisely in the glyphs there (& they are the best there are, on

all counts, both calendar & art) that the fish gets drawn most accurately.

I can't resist setting down one shot I made this morning, talking with Con, which, I think, opens out in several directions. I was complaining, that I have not been able to find, that any of these birds start with the simplest of a proposition when they are going on about the question, whether the glyphs were a language or not. I was saying, if they agree that the chronicles (The Books of Chilam Balam) rest on records previous to themselves (as do the codices, definitely), then, why don't they tell us—or just ask—what kind of an alphabet was it that preceded the Spanish letters in which Maya has been written since the Conquest (it is in our alphabet that the Books of Chilam Balam are written). The question answers itself: it was in hieroglyphs (the codices supplying the answer). So all that's left to answer is, was the invention of a written use contemporary, or later than, the use of same on stone? And by god if Thompson doesn't let the whole thing fall into place, without knowing it, so far as I can see now, when he tells this beautiful tale:

(preface: the codices are books, the paper was the wild fig beaten thin, and then coated with a wash of lime on which the colors and figures were "written"—and a book was as *y & x* was originally designed, that is, one continuous sheet of this paper (the longest known being the Codex Madrid, about 20 feet!), folded as was *y & x*, the text running left to right on "pages" abt 5 inches tall & 2½ to 3 inches wide and the same left to right on the back, the book completing itself on the back of page 1: many of the pages are simply in red and black on the white lime, but in some places the details or backgrounds are in blue-green, light & dark yellow, brown, red, pink, black, all of several tones). ok.

Very destructible. Only three survived. However, sometimes codices were buried with the so-called "priests," or the learned men, which, still, I'd prefer to call 'em,

107

until I know what this was they talk abt as "religion."
anyhow.

At this point T writes: "This information—that the codices
were buried with 'em—has been confirmed by the discovery of
heaps of thin flakes of lime with painting on them in tombs at
Uaxactun and San Agustin Acasaguastlan. These surely represent the sizing of pages after the vegetal backings had disinte-
grated. A tomb at Nebaj yielded a codex in a slightly better
stage of presentation."

The point is, Uaxactun (I can't find where the other two were).
But Uaxactun is the oldest, or twin-oldest, of all the cities, and
was apparently not lived in after 889 A.D. (the date of its last
stela).

   Well, said, it doesn't seem to say much. But i smell it as
important, tho, just yet, i can't demonstrate (it opens up,
the fluency of, the glyphs, for me: which is what i have felt
in them since that first day i saw them through Sánchez's
drawings. and leads straight on in to the heart of their meaning
& design as language, not, as astrological pictographs
                                                   the distinc-
tion is, that it is necessary to separate the glyphs from the use
they were put to, that is, no argument, that the major use was,
to record in stone the investigations by the learned of time &
planets, but—because the stone has stayed, while another use—
for books, painted or written with a brush—has mostly disappeared, there is no reason not to come in quite fresh from the
other end, and see the whole business of glyphs as, 1st, language,
and, afterward, uses of same
                               and it is the fact that the glyphs
were the alphabet of the books that puts the whole thing back
to the spoken language. Or so it seems to me, this morning.

and with that established, it would seem that the Maya
language as we have had it since it got the Spanish alphabet

should be, by way of its sounds, the clue to the meanings of
that two-thirds of the glyphs which are still wholly unknown

I worked out, yesterday, this, as the method I'd like to follow:

the glyphs
(their design & rhythms, in addition to
what denotation the scholars have found)

the present Maya language	*all surviving tales, records,*
(for its sounds & meanings,	*"poems," songs etc: the "li-*
˙not its orthography)	*terature"* (Books of Chilam
	Balam, plus Codices, plus)

and that means as much Mexican Indian as Mayan (or, for
that matter, North American Indian, for you undoubtedly
tasted an old flavor in that tale of the moon i sent you yesterday,
eh?) ((I still prefer what Sumerians incised on clay!))

But all this is too fucking bearing down to bother you with.
Let me shut up, and, instead, shoot you, quick, other impres-
sions which have been coming in:

(1) that these Maya were a damned nice uncertain, uneasy,
nervous, fragile bunch of humans with eyes wide open,
and jumpy, like a bird or animal, in the midst of, themselves as creatures and the seasons & the stars—(ex., the
way the sun, moon, venus come out, in that story; and
all over the place the way they never set anything sym-
metrical, even, the sun (don't know, but just wonder if,
those peoples who plug the sun aren't always, warriors,
cutthroats, like the late Mexican (aztecs, or, even
earlier, the chichemecs)

((another: at Copan only *one* glyph with the head of a
snake split open, and the design made as the Alaskans
did it, by the symmetry of, such, a paper cut-out—in

other words the danger, the stereotype, of the very formalism of which the maya were masters

on the other hand, the way, the glyphs never got out of hand (out of media) as did the architecture & the pots, running, to naturalism, say, the danger of the other side, the openness, the intimate)) the way they kept the abstract alert

& (2) time: Copan D answers, for me, the whole contradiction I had felt, fr that fact that Morley & the rest keep blowing bubbles, abt, ah, the mayah, and time-ah! shit, sd i: no people i'm committed to could be devoted to time as these loose-heads say they were, but i knew no answer, and, surely they did spend a hell of a lot of time on time, surely

but the first chance i get, and can get a copy of Copan D to send you, will, so that you can see, that time, in their minds, was *mass & weight!* and they even doubled the onus, making, in Copan D, as well as generally, making the *number* of the given time unit (20, say, of 20 days) the carrier of the burden of, the unit itself! that is, Copan D is a date 9 baktuns (400 yrs)

15 katuns (20 yrs)
5 tuns (year of 360)
0 uninal (month of 20 days)
0 kin (day)

3905 yrs total

it is pictured thus:

man 9 carrying baktun (a huge zopalote) on his back (as the woodsmen still carry their baskets, by the band across their forehead)

man 15 wrestling with katun (same vulture, only, clawing)

110

man 5 somewhat pleased with himself
for now carrying a dead vulture over
his shoulder

etc.

well, lad, i'll quit, go for a swim, eat and shove off again for
Campeche for another session with Sánchez over his drawings:
we get a solid two hours in, working them over, together—and
it's good, damned good . . .

13

sunday   april 1

. . . What continues to hold me, is, the tremendous levy on all
objects as they present themselves to human sense, in this glyph-
world. And the proportion, the distribution of weight given
same parts of all, seems, exceptionally, distributed & accurate,
that is, that

     sun
          moon
               venus
                         other constellations & zodiac
     snakes
           ticks
              vultures
     jaguar
          owl
              frog
     feathers
             peyote
                  water-lily
     not to speak of
     fish
          caracol
             tortoise

```
                 &, above all,
                 human eyes
                     hands
                       limbs        (PLUS EXCEEDINGLY
                                     CAREFUL OBSERVA-
                                     TION OF ALL POSSI-
                                     BLE INTERVALS OF
                                     SAME, as well as ALL
                                     ABOVE (to precise di-
                                     mension of eclipses, say,
                                     & time of, same etc. etc.)
```

And the weights of same, each to the other, is, immaculate
(as well as, full)

That is, the gate to the center was, here, as accurate as what you
& i have been (all along) talking about—viz., man as object
in field of force declaring self as force because is force in exactly
such relation & can accomplish expression of self as force by
conjecture, & displacement in a context best, now, seen as space
more than a time such;

                          which, I take it, is precise contrary to,
what we have had, as "humanism," with, man, out of all proportion of, relations, thus, so mis-centered, becomes, dependent
on, only, a whole series of "human" references which, so made,
make only anthropomorphism, and thus, make mush of, *any*
reality, conspicuously, his own, not to speak of, how all other
forces (ticks, water-lilies, or snails) become only descriptive
objects in what used to go with antimacassars, those, plane-
tariums (ancestors of gold-fish bowls) etc.

This gate got to, gone in by, 2nd stage, follows, that is, *invention* produces narration & verse also of a contrary order (the
last example of which, which comes down to us, being,
ODYSSEY

             which, for my dough, is not good enough (ditto
only modern example i know, one melville), simply because
humanism is (homer) coming in, and (melville) going out

112

and i take it, a Sumer poem or Maya glyph is more pertinent to our purposes than anything else, because each of these people & their workers had forms which unfolded directly from content (sd content itself a disposition toward reality which understood man as only force in field of force containing multiple other expressions

one delightful fact, just picked up: that *all* Mayan jobs (sez Tatiana Proskouriakoff) are built around *a single human figure*, in all reliefs, etc.

which is, of course, that ego which you, me, Mayan X were (are), he who is interested enough to, seeing it all, get something down

What has to be battered down, completely, is, that this has anything to do with stage of development. Au contraire. The capacity for (1) the observation & (2) the invention has no more to do with brick or no wheels or metal or stone than you and i are different from, sd peoples: we are like. Therefore, there is no "history." (I still keep going back to, the notion, this is (we are) merely, the *second time* (that's as much history as I'll permit in, which ain't history at all: seems so, only, because we have been all dragooned into a notion that, what came between was, better. Which is eatable shit, for the likes of those who like, same.

Animation of what presents itself, fr the thing on outwards: rock as vessel, vessel as tale, creating, men & women, because narrator and/or poet happen to be man or woman, thus, human figure as part of universe of things

(Other things, of same, the provocations, say:

the *eye*, in Mayan (other Indian as well) & Sumerian fixes (jesus, in these glyphs, how, or stones, how, with *any* kind of device, the eye takes up life (contra Greek, Rome, even, Byzantine): ex.,

113

Museo, Campeche, a wonderful little "monster" with eyes made so

and the hands (fingers):
>   this is peculiarly brilliant at Copan
(as I sd), where, if any dancer now living had sense, he'd be,
finding out, how, to exploit this part of his, instrument
>   not to speak of how the face is, the other domi-
>   nant glyph in addition to the abstracts of all
>   other natural forms, is, the human or animal
>   *heads* . . .

14

friday april 6 (It's 3 P.M., at which hour I have just had break-
fast, which may be a gauge, the 15 hrs, of the toll of woods &
ruins: two days, & a day of preparation for same—Con not able
to go along, so, alone, whatever better than 200 kilometers is,
away fr here. And the craziest of it, being, put up, the night
before last in a jail! At Santa Elena, the very town, it turned
out afterwards, where Stephens based himself, 100 yrs agone,
when he hit same sites:

Uxmal & Kabah   (((found out, it's tick poisoning,
>   which, I've had: you shld not be
>   me, this morning, with my trunk
>   wholly raised in sores, plus, fr
>   the jail water, tourista, viz, GIs:
>   up at 6 this morning))) . . .

lerma   campeche   monday   april 23   51

. . . Bushed, hoy. And precisely the verb. For, the bush, of
Jaina, leaves me so. Jesus, what a job these lands are, in the sun!
Impossible, the way, the sun drags you down—in one half hr
it is eating you, its clawing having pulled you off yr pins.
Wicked. I tried, for awhile, to scratch away at the walls of the
graves (one leaps in to holes which are exactly like the stage
holes into which Hamlet leaps). But there, with what breeze
there is coming fr the sea (and there was good breeze yesterday)
cut off, one can't take more than 5 minutes! I'm telling you,
lad, one thing is hugely proved: one can't touch this Yucatan
(or I'd gather, any place of these Maya) without full expeditionary equipment. Which, of course, means, institutions. Ergo,
mal.

Any one place requires, instantly, two to three days: that
is, all one can do the first day, is to get there. For by that time
the sun is too far up to do anything but sleep in some place out
of the sun. So that evening, and the next morning, early, are
the only work times. Which means, almost, the 3rd day, for
return. All of which is too expensive for the likes of one sole
adventurer as me!

We got away at 5 A.M., the lad, who was to sail us, having, I
guess, spent too long at the baile the night before, for, tho we
were up before 4, the two of us, he didn't show until almost
five.

The run was lovely: 4 hrs, with a strong following wind,
so strong the cayuco, in the hour before the sun came, was
heeled over so, her gunwale was taking water! And by god if
Con wasn't way the hell out in front of me, taking it! And it
her first time in a fisherman! Tho I shld say, she knows sailing
boats, I, never, previously, having been under sail except in
schooners. Wonderful rich sea. And after, with the wind losing

that first freshness, under double sail, going like hell across the gulf, straight run, almost due north fr here: a fine lad, 24, 10 yrs fisherman, without grace, but handling his boat confidently.

Hit Jaina abt 9:30, left at 3:00. So it was the meanest part of the day that we had to work. Result: no chance to take away—to find any of the great clays with which the whole "island" is soaked: it is, its whole length & width (approximately a circle, diameter abt half a mile), a cemetery: in fact, the water has intruded on the land on the seaward side considerably, and in the waters offshore one can spot the tell-tale scattering of pieces of pots (literally, as the lady sd, like, rose-petals, literally, color and all—as tho the Maya brought boatloads and threw handfuls as some sort of a gesture of farewell or protection to those, they buried there).

Craziest damn thing ever, this place: nothing on it otherwise but two sets of double small pyramids at either end of the "island": one to seaward, one toward the land (now, of course, just rounded hills). And not even raisings where the graves are, as, say, like "ours"! Just a flat island, abt like (with the two raised ends looking, fr seaward, as dunes) coming on the coast, there, abt Ipswich, say! Only difference, that, the shore is, mangrove.

But here's the punch-line: a damned attractive place, as place, so much so it occurred to both C & me, was it the reason the Maya (from wherever they came to this jut of the land driving out into the sea just here, to bury their, dead) did so come here, choose, this place?

Must find out more. There've been 3 expeditions to dig same, and, the 1st I imagine, found a glyph stone here with the date 652 A.D. Which is one of the earliest dates known north of Guatemala. And long before the building of the major cities of the north. Know no bibliography on the place, only, one lousy book Pavon & a guy named Pina Chan did, on the graves, 3 yrs ago. (Figure on this, as on so many things, I shall have to find out by reading reports in the Instituto Nacional in Mex City, where, all mss of expeditions are collected.)

I'd guess one thing: if we had gone up there when we first came, I'm sure I'd have wanted to promote us a singleteam expeditionary force to live there awhile, and dig. For it has the damndest charm, the place. And one roofless building at the landing (dating back to Spanish 18th century) in which to live with an ancient well there in which the loveliest doves (very small, no more than five inches overall) hide.

I slept, awhile, on the return, folded in under the thwarts, out of the sun which had spent me, and fitting the bottom just like one of its knees: it was a throwback, for me, to the way it was sleeping, in a schooner's peak, with the water's sounds coming in through the wood of the planks . . .

One can buy one of these cayucos, complete with double sails, for 250 bucks! And the rest of the time back Con and I played with the notion of borrowing some such dough to buy same and to return to the States so! (Turned out it would take two months, the lad sd, just to get, by the coast, to Vera Cruz!) But what an idea, eh? And fine, while it lasted!

Well. Just to keep you, in. Am weak like sick, and so no words, hoy. But damned happy to have been there: if you had seen any of these small clay figures they buried clutched in the hands of their dead, you'd know why. They are intimate, close human things, these—what the dopes call—"anthropomorphic" figurines. Jesus. Or "zoomorphic"! And two (here in the Museum) are those I guess I must have mentioned to you: of the calyx of clay with little humans sitting where the pistil might be?

And no telling what else is there, the place has not been really dug at all: a couple of halfhearted "trenchings" of the pair of pyramids. And spotted exhumations of, the graves (the

117

graves go right to the mangrove edge! must have been dug right
in salt water!

what bend of mind motivated this
place? from how far did the people come who came here to bury?
how did they come, by sea? for tho the "island" is only more
of the land furruled by breakings in of, water, there is nothing
inside to indicate any human settlements for great distances.
damned funny, the whole, business (and, so far as I know, no
other similar example anywhere among the Maya, tho, I should
have liked very much to have gone around to the East coast &
seen Isla Mujeres, Cozumel, and Tulum, over there, where, the
Maya were coastal and thick. . . .

16

sun apr 29 51

. . . for RC:

	(architecture)	(ceramica)	(date)
EARLY DEVELOPMENTAL	PRE-MASONRY	MAMOM	? (1000 yrs) ?
LATE DEVELOPMENTAL	PRE-VAULT	CHICANEL	? ditto-278 A.D.

((in EARLY, no buildings, much flint, & pottery figurines;
in LATE, 1st formal plaza idea, but, only at very
end, truncated pyramids (with wood superstruc-
tures), & no pot. figs.))

EARLY CLASSIC	VAULT I	TZAKOL	278-593 A.D.

(1) glyphs (2) stone superstructs. (3) burials, in crypts,
instead of just turned up, ground (4) many-colors,
on pots (5) jade

(meaning, the climax of,
building) stone for veneer,
the carefully cut pieces we
find at our cuyo thin walls,

wider windows, bigger
rooms

abandonment of site, even tho site still top shape!

for Ann:

as against the agronomy explanations of, the abandonment
of, the southern cities, AVKidder argues, excellently, that it
won't hold (either (1) that they maized-out, the soil, or (2) that
they cut off so many zapote trees, they got erosion, & silted up
their lakes into malaria swamps), simply because such sites as
Quirigua (on the river Montagua, which, floods like the Nile,
offsetting either of above explanations, obviously) and the Usu-
macinta sites (river, again: Piedras Negras, Palenque) *were also
deserted when*, the other, inlands, were! Copan, likewise! which
sits, even today, ready, for, occupancy

for SB:

Uaxactun answers, on water: had exact reservoirs, very much
the same as, ours ((see Ricketson & Ricketson, 1937, Carnegie
                    Pub. 477, pp. 9-11; & A. Ledyard Smith,
                    1950, same, No. 588, pp. 61, 84))

natural clay removed to depth of (in one case, the smaller of
two, 7½ feet at center) and graded to surrounding ground level

the bottom had then been covered with 3 inch deposit of sand
on which was laid a pavement of large stone slabs which, in
turn, were covered by a 7 inch layer of sand (Late Classic)

the larger, is an almost circular one, about 100 feet in diameter and better than 16 feet deep! With a dam of natural ravine to feed in water on that side, and,—by god, on the other—on the side towards the causeway joining the two elements of the city which the pros. call Group A and Group B, if, by god, these lads hadn't cut a sluice in the parapet of the causeway so that, all drainage from all inclined city squares flowed, during the rainy season—the agua lluvia one hears these present people talking abt like they talk abt the weather these dry days (they have to pay 30 centavos a water vase for it, just abt now, fr., big shots with, exactly the same inclined run-offs, hereabouts, now, individually owned, and charged for, contra, then, eh?)—a SPILLWAY, no less, constructed (by the evidence of the pot fragments in the fill, just above, the bedrock) Early Classic, that is, between 300 and 600 A.D.

ok

17

sunday   july 1

. . . the thing on my mind today is, a feeling, that this would be a damned good place to be the hell out of the mess which I expect to grow worse up there to the north, as well as generally in Europe and Asia, the next few years . . .

The point is, a double one: (1) that I have, somehow, to work out an economic "modo" to pay me while I write verse, anywhere, and (2) that a buck, here, works at least three times as hard. And if this Indian stuff can be made to do it, I don't think of a better jointure. For their nouns, undone, are my nouns.
    Ex: Alfonso
    (Mariano's 7 yr old brother) came up with this yesterday. His brother-in-law is a farmer, back in the hills.

And that toc bird—the one I may have described to
you, that picks its own tail away to beautify itself (or
so Stromsvik taught me), leaving the end only, which is
a peacock's eye—troubles this poor farmer, troubles him
so, he stones them because, says he, can't look into the
mirror of that tail, it frightens him, so he has to smash
it!

Which goes right to the heart of the matter. For that
damned bird just does use its tail as though it were a
mirror, switching it around like proud lady does her
own—for admiration!

What would lay you in the aisles, is a Sunday (today), to see
these fishermen (7–13), after six days in cayucos with their pas
or older brothers, real live cayucos on real live gulf with goddamned dangerous northers coming off the American continent,
or, this season, chubascos loaded with rain from the east (from
the trades, and their collision with this thumb of land, the
peninsula), running or swimming up and down the beach here
outside me sailing their own-made toy cayucos! Damndest mix-
up ever. The same lads you'd have seen last night, with white
shirts buttoned up in that queer old-fashioned shallow collar,
taking the night air with their fellow fishermen, their elders, on
the plaza—doing everything the others do of a Saturday night
except get drunk on the bad rum and good beer!

There is this lad, 9, who, for the past two years,
has, as the oldest in his family, his father dead,
somehow managed to bring in 6 pesos a day. And
now fishes, probably taking 10, say, a day—and
thus the principal support now, that he is a fisherman. Or is he 11, and has been doing it since 9?
Maybe that's it. But what the hell—the scale is
crazy, however you look at it.

And by god none of them get enough to eat, even
so. And I do not mean by gorging American com-

parisons. By minimums. 4 eggs, for example, for an omelet for a family of 7! (This is the hardest part of it here, the business, of what we buy, as against them, to maintain our own habits—which, despite my size, are nothing compared to my fellow cits. It bothers Con so much she will hand over the money to me to keep from giving it away! Or will buy less pork than she wants, or less oranges, from the eyes which watch her at the store!

There is one guy, Chica, whom we do not know enough to peg. He seems to be employed by the town, for odd jobs. But he is poor, whether from laziness, as Chappy says, or from the disabilities of scarlet fever (is it?) or malaria, as others say. In any case, he is a shrewd beggar, and has a nose to hang at the door of the store just when Con has to cash a 50 peso bill! The other day, she just couldn't do it, and though she had shown the bill to the store people, she asked, in the end, seeing Chica, to charge what she had bought! But fortunately, the time he hit me, hard, I gave in. I looked out the window (some distance from the door at which he had knocked) and sure enough, there was, at the door, a woman who he sd was his wife, and she did have, as I could see from the lump in her rebozo, what he said was their baby, who was sick, he sd, and would I give him 5 pesos to take it to a doctor. Thank God. For though it did not save the thing's life, it was that sick, he did have the chance to have it get the injections which they all believe, around here, is what solves all troubles!

Even to our medicines, we have these people "conquered," god help them.

It's just the last remnant of the older life—that life which had been man's way all that time until our generation—that gives this place still its resonance. This morning, it was too much, to wake to the sort of noises which they make here the day they don't work, and set out for chicharrons (pork scraps) which are the day's delicacy. Or last night to go off for ice, and be confronted, on the main street, with a horse racing toward me in the street-light dark, and not being able to figure out what the hell is the light thing riding it, until, they are almost on me, and I have to squeeze up against the building, by this time knowing, and nervous, they'll shy, for it's a stallion mounting her, and going like hell the two of them, scaring the old ladies in their rockers out on the sidewalk, and all the guys at the square roaring with laughter at this invasion from the country!

Con figures, the animals, can't any more resist Saturday night in town—paseo, Senor y Senora, pasanado?—than any of us can. Every Saturday night—and no other night, by god, if three goats don't come in and chew their way through it all! And precisely ma, pa, and little goat! Exactly like a Maya family in, from the farms, back of Quila!

It's crazy. And to feel the crash of the American noises blot out these other older things! The buses and trucks and convertibles, the Birdseye freezing plant's generators, and the planes! It's—here—being on the divide, precisely at watershed.

And it has a personal wallop. For it puts me almost exactly where things were, in the States, when I was etc. Crazy, to feel that same bouncing, from yourself! Damned refreshing.

Don't but see but what we are the legitimate bearers of value, simply because, we have known it, both ways, the first, to so know what men can do. To cut in, right there, where what was can be coolly known, and what is, can be separated from, hope: what a spot! Like it, myself, and think we damn well have the advantage of our elders—and better use same, instead, as I mostly observe, fall back (even Ez, the greatest) or fall on our face, as most. (Again, DHL, seems the only one who, didn't mug either, who, stood there, getting it, as his own).

Well, lad, from Lerma then, no goodbye, but just, in passing, the word. The "Lucero di Alba" is now reported for tomorrow, which means we ought to be off about Thursday, the 5th, is it, getting us to Pensacola the 8th—or a day or so later, I'd guess, knowing the stevedores in this hyar port. So we'll be a couple of days late arriving at North Carolina, not that it matters. Except that I shall be hungry for some mail from you. Keep it piling up, please. I should like to make the switch without breaking stride, but that, surely, is a fool's dream . . .

* * *

BIBLIOGRAPHY

"The scientific bias taken by our civilization has . . . given to History and Archeology a role, valuable and respectable, of course, but not inspired."

—Edward Hyams,
Soil & Civilization
(Thames & Hudson, 1952)

(1) in such a category:

J. Eric S. Thompson, *Mayan Hieroglyphic Writing: Introduction*
(Carnegie Institution, 1950)

THE MAYA AND THEIR NEIGHBORS, essays in honor of Alfred Tozzer (D. Appleton-Century, 1940), especially Oliver G. Ricketson Jr.'s "Outline of Basic Physical Factors Affecting Middle

America"; also Earnest Hooton's de-
bunking of sacrifice by analysis of
skeletons from the Cenote at Chichen Itza

A. V. KIDDER's hypothesis of civil
war as explanation of the "deserted
cities," in his introduction of the
Carnegie publication of the work of
the Smiths at Uaxactun &—merely
to have the glyphs to look at, and in
lieu of any existing publication of
the drawings from the glyphs by
Hippolito Sánchez—Morley's *The
Inscriptions at Copan,* and *The Inscriptions of Peten* (Carnegie Institution, 1920, 1937-38)

The climax still, of all such work is Bulletin
No. 28 of the Bureau of American Ethnology,
24 papers on "Mexican and Central American
Antiquities" by Seler, Forstemann, Schellhas,
Sapper and Dieseldorff, edited by Bowditch
(Washington, Government Printing Office,
1904)

(2)   not so respectable,
      but stabs at value,
      on the language question:

the long work of William E. Gates,
from 1910 to 1940, published by the
Maya Society, Baltimore, and including his outline dictionary of
Maya glyphs, 1931;
                    &—though here
I am as doubting as Thompson is
choleric—B. L. Whorf's four papers

on Maya, among his many on other languages, and on language itself.

(*Note:* how questionable Whorf's work is may be judged by the free ride it is just now getting from those sinister rightists, the semantic people, who come out of that "human engineering" one, Non-A Korzybski)

(3) Neither Archaeology nor History, but the only intimate and active experience of the Maya yet in print:

JOHN L. STEPHENS, two books, *Incidents of Travel in Central America, Chiapas, and Yucatan* (N. Y., 1841), and *Incidents of Travel in Yucatan* (N. Y., 1843), with Frank Catherwood's drawings in each, of *ruinas,* and of the stelae, for checking against Sánchez. (Prescott and Parkman are a triad: Stephens is the unacknowledged third.)

Also—a guess on my part—the scattered work, and unpublished manuscripts, of ROBERT BARLOW, dead, by his own hand, January, 1951

II

"This 'poet's technique' has rarely been applied to the study of the past

127

and perhaps never to the study of
the remote past."

—Hyams, op. cit.
(the preceding sentence to previous
quote from him)

D. H. Lawrence did. And Melville, before him:

ex., Lawrence, preface, FANTASIA
OF THE UNCONSCIOUS, where
he imagines states of being & geography divers from the modern

Nor is it a "technique." It is disposition, to reality. And can be
precisely known, as is.

But the matter here is to isolate the works of these two men as
the only ones who have so "applied," "to the study of," since
Herodotus ("History" came into being with Herodotus's exact
contemporary, Thucydides), and to go on to discriminate other
works which, because they are of the past as it is not merely
History or Archaeology, enable one to give the Maya the present
they once were, and are:

Brooks Adams, *The New Empire*
(N. Y., 1902, with maps), for the
scope of its trade-and-money story,
even if eventually any of his work is
boring from the capitulation in him
to the machine as sufficient analogy
for all process

Leo Frobenius' books on Africa,
Rock Paintings, and Paideuma, despite questions; his "Childhood of
Man," one of his earliest, is still, so
far as I know, the only one trans-
lated into English.

Jane Harrison, anything of hers,
notably (for me) *PROLEGO-*

MENA *to the Study of Greek Religion*

Pausanias's *Description of Greece,* more valuable than Plutarch, his immediate predecessor, c. 100 A.D., because of its careful localism, and taking what is said as how to find out for oneself

Ezra Pound, *Guide to Kulchur,* just because it razzledazzles History. And any Learning. But its loss is exactly that. Plus the poet's admitted insistence he will stay inside the Western Box, Gemisto, 1429 A.D., up

Carl O. Sauer, "Environment and Culture in the Deglaciation," American Philosophical Society, 1947, the single gate to the remote past; see also his "American Agricultural Origins: A Consideration of Nature and Culture," in Essays in Anthropology in Honor of Alfred Kroeber (Berkeley, 1936)

(Addendum, Attic, Annex, Any hidden place:

for those who have the wit to tell the Unconscious when they see one, or for the likes of me, who was raised on the American Weekly, there are at least two men I want to mention (not to speak of Ignatius Donnelly on Atlantis, Churchward on Mu— or, for that matter, Rider Haggard!):

the Frenchman, Victor Berard, Mediterranean explorer, who wrote several books to show that the *Odyssey* was a rewrite from a Semitic original; and a Scot, L. A. Waddell, also an explorer, of Tibet, who was sure that the Sumerians or the Hittites or the Trojans founded the British Hempire, and that Menes the Egyptian was Minos the Cretan and ended up dead, from the bite of a wasp, in Ireland, at Knock-Many, the "Hill of Many," in County Tyrone.

But no one but an herodotean may fool around with such fraudulence & fantasy practiced on document (instead of on the galaxies), no matter how much such stories are, to my taking, the body of narrative which has intervened between the great time of fiction & drama (the City-time) and the present (which is no time for fantasy, drama—or City).

The trouble is, it is very difficult, to be both a poet and, an historian.

October, 1953

III

APOLLONIUS OF TYANA

A Dance, with Some Words, for Two Actors

The dancer, Apollonius
The voice, Tyana, or place

The Introduction, or
THE GAMBIT

Some light should come on, before the first words of the
introduction are spoken, but it should be small light, and
slow over the general area, only enough to decrease the
original blackness to the condition of shadow among rocks
or in a mountain pass when the day is off west. A very
white stick of light then picks out from the general ob-
scurity a hump about two-thirds of the way back on an
oblique axis from the audience. It is the two actors, sitting
on the floor faces front, the dancer close inside the legs of
Tyana, so close as to obscure the body and head of the
other actor.

As Tyana speaks the introduction most slowly and most
clearly, it should be as though the words came out of the
mouth of the forward figure, the dancer—whose lips do not
move, or his features, at first, they are held, and it is like
a soliloquy in the cinema, with the face steady and the
words coming from the sound track, like thoughts alongside the concentration.

As the introduction proceeds, however, the dancer should
discover movement, first of his face, then of his fingers,
until the most dramatic discovery for him is his two arms.
And when he raises them out and to the side, Tyana, too,
should accompany him, so that, at a high moment, they
compose together a four armed figure.

133

As the introduction comes to its ending, a two armed, two legged man is erect, the single dancer himself, ready to move off, to make his next discoveries in space. (There is no reason why, for a split second, timed to the content of the speech, he should not be the classic proportional figure of man, bound by a circle, legs and arms spread to cut the circle into four arcs—a sudden geometric and annunciative man measurer and to be measured.

As and when Apollonius moves off, Tyana swings to an easy reclining position, indolent, you might say, lying like a confident thing, on one elbow, and watching all movements of the dancer, constantly pushing and pulling the dancer away and towards herself, by traction, through concentration. And there will be moments when Tyana will fall back, as though into sleep, leaving Apollonius free, leaving all attention solely on the dance.)

Tyana:

It is not remembered that three of the chief of men were born pretty much at the same time: Buddha, Confucius, Lao-Tze, three places three men, three of men who were not content with what had been, who found it necessary to shape themselves with greater accuracy than had been men's wont, at least in their time, to try to make more sense out of experience than ambience alone ever allows.

Let me detach your minds from religion. Let me, instead, direct your minds to birth, how men, once born, seek to be born another way—and without necessary reference to such words as "spirit" or "the after-life." In other words, let me remind you that men, first, deal with their lives, their discoveries therein—in their own and other lives—and that they seek by their actions, if they are serious men, to concentrate their own and others' attentions to the closer intervals, not of any removed place but of the intervals which surround us here, here in the distraction of the present and the obvious, in short, that which surrounds us, what we make, what we live in and by and (not so often) for—as such as these did live, as such as he lived whom I want here to tell you most about, a man whom here and now I am offering to you anew.

His name is mostly forgotten. But there are reasons, political reasons that, since the 3rd Century of the Christian era, since the Empress Domna Julia wanted to know more about him, no one has heard much about him, even though there was a time when he was as known as his twin, that twin you well know, whom I, in fact, because I am a Cappadocian, would say you know too well, too little and too well, one Jesus Christ.

I wish you only to note how men spring up, when they are needed, like violets, on all sides, in the spring, when the winter has been too long. 500 years after Buddha, Confucius, Lao-Tze, two men sprang up: the Christ, to honor him as you do, and this man, to whom I now call your attention. They were born very close to the same time and not so very far apart in space (in space, that thing which means so much to me as a force, more than it does seem to mean to you) 500 air miles, say—like you say, so easily—north north east of where Christ was born; and in an area mostly now forgotten or thought of as where Turks are or some other dark-skinned people who peddle rugs, or better, pieces of carpet, and have round spots on their cheeks like vaccinations.

It is curious about ignorance, how it thrives—even ignorance of such a common thing, such an easily found out thing as the contours and peoples of what any of us share, the earth. Or ignorance, for that matter, of time—what has gone on in time amongst others as well as yourselves, you who have quarrelled largely, have moved from civil war of farming brothers to civil war of all of us—and for what? for peace, for petroleum, the newest silly sediment.

But there you are. Even your newest war of the world comes home to me, comes to me the center of what was anciently the world and is now again—and just in such terms as resources and war—the center of the world. But I am a Cappadocian and as a child of the Caucasus Mountains (as you all, actually, are), I do not propose to offer anything but what you used to be able to deal with so firmly: facts. It is time now, as it always is, to put aside ambiguities. I shall not let issue from myself by one hair or fissure of myself the slightest ambiguity, any double-talk. For you are not here for riddles. The answer, in fact, is always, was always, the simplest, even though it may, for so many, stay riddle. If there is any truth at all, it is only you yourself, you who was born on four legs, who found out how to walk on two and who would wish—who hopes—so to manage his strength that he will stay erect, will not have to come down to end as we all began, almost on all fours. At least you will try to avoid being so forced down hill that you will not have to, like some Australian creature, go to the grave on three.

How shall you manage it? You see, ascension is an invention. Gotama Buddha, one day, lay down to die, and after telling his closest friends, and those flies his disciples, that he was about to die, they, pressing on him for some final message, the fools, heard what any wise man should remind his fellows: that they, too, had work to do to shape themselves before they too died as he was dying, and that that shape they only could fashion, out of themselves, that he was no more than a man who had spent his time doing his fashioning, that was all. In other words, the tale I have to tell has a beginning and an end.

So let us begin. Let me show you something of this man of my own place, something remarkable on him like a coast has things which stand out like a white house or a clump of trees, some such thing which has not heretofore been revealed of this man who moved off from me, from Tyana where he was born, who moved most gradually from this center out as far as a man then could go

and does it matter how far, so long as it is far, as far as any particular man can go?

can you say how far far is? can you think of any man of all these I have mentioned who (except for Gotama, perhaps) moved as far as you shall see this man move, as far as, indeed, so far as space goes, as you too have the opportunity to move do you recall that even Kung Fu Tse had not, he admitted, been as far as Tai, the precious mountain?

and certainly you do know how local Christ was.

There are two things to be said about this Apollonius of mine, of Tyana, two things he was most aware of, more aware of, certainly, than any one but one other man, perhaps, in all the time since, of all the men who have been busy, in that time, about human business.

I don't mean to press you too hard. Let me be quiet and direct. I want you only to recognize that far is not so very far, and that my lad, this Apollonius knew, as I say, two important things: ONE, that how is it far if you think of it, but, TWO, that far could not well be less than that you think of it yet it must be more and that to find out how more one must MOVE.

And so he moved, off from me, he moved as only, before him, from my mountains the race moved, Buddha moved, and since, man has—well, he has migrated but still, who, among you, has so moved?

MOVE *one*

Apollonius moves, as slowly as he discovered his limbs, off gradually to stage left, in other words south south west, to ANTIOCH. And when he does arrive at this first limit, the lighting should define the whole segment of that geography, in a color special to itself and the wall of the color abrupt, like a jig-saw slice—in order that each of the moves to follow shall add themselves by the action of Apollonius' dance until the whole stage area is transformed into the ancient world, from India to Cadiz, a colored "map" of it, with the Mediterranean the axis, and that axis oblique to the audience, in other words running from upper stage left to lower stage right. If possible the colors should come on as outlines of coasts simultaneously with Apollonius' movements as those movements define those coasts or, where it is inland, new topographies—in other words, the feeling, both of the movement of the man and the color should be the creation both of periploi (charts of coasts) and of topographical maps.

Tyana:

He left me, first, for Antioch: a man cannot abide for long the place of his birth, the place of his first experience, the thing is too close for him to know, not what it is, but how to gauge it. And besides, there is the body, the physical thing, it has to be explored. For in what sense is it not the base of the legend? And yet is it not, strangely, what we know least about, this huge earth we know less about than we even know of the other, the larger one? of these mountains of kidneys which can suddenly crumble, of this Great Lakes of the liver, of this Tigris and Euphrates system the heart, which can so easily break and then there is death, of these Neocene bones, the geology of ourselves, which live longest, of this seed and strange cotyledon, the brain, of these flowers and grasses which can be cut off, the fingers? What do we guess of our own functions and of their most private life, their dangers—despite all our speculation about arrowheads, or storms in nebulae, or whether Africa or Asia was where an ape got the use of his thumb, or the use of fire?

The thing is, Apollonius was interested, 1st, that when man invented a city he got important (so far as we, the children of cities are concerned) and 2nd, that healing, any kind of healing, like any kind of usable discovery, starts with the human body, its complicated and animal structure, what the masters he first went to understood to rest in *kinesis.*

The dance of Antioch is *the dance of the body,* and the body as first part of the way. His masters were of the Aesculapian-Pythagorean school, and had drawn out of the ancient world disciplines for the body and its health which rested on the concept that to heal it is necessary first to know, and that to know is more than mechanics, however much any knowing of the body must rest on a complete knowledge of its behavior. It is a concept we have only known the ragged end of, and so we have doctors for the mind and doctors for the body and neither of them know what a dancer now has to know, or a composer, or a poet, if any of these latter craftsmen are honestly attacking their craft.

What Apollonius was first taught was, that how a tree sways is as much of the matter as is how you sway; how any hanging thing is as you hang by the hook of gravitation, hang, as a pendulum swings: how, to heal, is also how you eat and how you find out how—somehow—to maintain your resistance (of which act secrecy is an honest part, his Pythagorean teachers taught him).

And he said, Apollonius said, it was his conclusion, that what he got from Antioch was, how to act fiercely but, with dignity.

And he ate no animal food and he wore nothing made of animal skin. Blood seemed to him of consequence. His feeling was, that man has no right to use anything but what, like a crop or the wool of a sheep, can grow again—like trees can grow, if top soil is not the price paid for cutting a stand off, as war cuts off men after their mothers can bear again

Apollonius speaks:
How do you differ yourselves from how you eat, eh? How do you make a god (which is the same as how do you make an image of yourself) without making him all maw, as you yourselves are, with your body unknown and merely set off, like an eating machine, by some button, as you set war off?
How are you anything but a hole in the earth?

And he moved on.

MOVE *two*
First, he returned home, to Tyana. His father had died, and left him and his brother the family wealth. Apollonius

139

resigned his share of the patrimony. It was not difficult for him. He put it very quietly. He said,

> I give it away to those who desire such
> things. Naked I seek the Naked.

It was no more and no less a decision than Gotama's, the only difference, obviously, that Apollonius did not have such a struggle over the world. Perhaps, as it is now, the world was not so attractive, and the decision was easier than it was for Gotama who had a white horse and such a handsome wife and child.

When Apollonius moved off again, he went south south east, down the two old rivers of the East, to BAGDAD. We have forgotten what any Arab knows, that Bagdad, for all the long years—the centuries—after the collapse of man's first disciplines (man's first cities), Bagdad remained the intellectual center, the old intellectual center, and much more in touch with the nerve ends of the old path than Alexandria ever was, or than the newest Alexandria, your Manhattan is, today, any clue to the path, the path which doesn't die, the path which is no more than yourself, if you can find it.

Apollonius did a natural thing, to start to find it, but not an easy thing, especially for a gregarious man. And surely Apollonius was no monk, as you shall discover, was no thin fellow without a roar in his chest. He was no bull, that is also true, but he was loaded with an appetite for the real world, the world we forget is the world as we love it—the world of other men. He craved to talk, as any live man does, to get at things by talking about them. In fact, he was one of those who talked to live. But he came quickly on a danger: that it is not easy to keep talk from sliding into small talk and at the same time it is not easy for talk to avoid (in order to avoid small talk) parables, anecdotes, all those easy stoppages of conversation which pass themselves off as wisdom sayings and are nothing more than schmerz, than, ah, how large life is and how long, which doesn't matter a breath to any live man, how his predecessors were eternal about it, it does not matter, he only wants to be sharp about it, to stay on its point, to hold all that it contains, not dissipate an ounce of it by any such generalizations, however couched in humor or weh. So Apollonius took a vow of silence for five years. He put this burden on himself, this bit. He said not one thing for five years. He listened, instead. He found out how to hear. He stripped himself of the heartiest thing of all, next to passion: he stopped the lively little animal, his tongue. He made his breath stay home. He wore his mind as firmly as, at Antioch, he had found out how to wear his body.

You can call it a descent, a sinking down into—as a poet, say, sinks—into (it is not easy to say what it is one sinks into) but it is surely clear what a blind place it is, and yet how, it is wholly related to light, to that which we identify with the light of the mind. The mind also has kinesis, and a large part of its behaviors are, like the body's, matters of struts and strains, and they take examination that speech, too easy a speech, loses the voice of, loses the body and breath of. So, again, he was an alert man, to take silence on while he mastered the things of the mind Bagdad had to offer him (the more overtly intellectual things—like languages, or engineering—in contrast to the geometry, the more hermetic knowledge he had before, of the Pythagoreans).

The dance, then, here in the gray and gold light of the FIRST VALLEY, is *the dance of the mind as a mute*—muted man and muted place: Tyana sits with her eyes and ears wide open (so Apollonius dances) but with a marvellous warmth and openness to the silent mouth (the mouth become as lips are which have the beauty of kiss—with no rattling, there, of the white teeth, those busy horses). Both actors should achieve, around their mouths, this richness which nobody knows any more, of how a river looks which moves winningly and doesn't say a word, of how eyes are

when the mind is clearly a clear thing and only doesn't
speak its content because it knows what apothegms never
quite get across—that however tragic is experience, it is
altogether beautiful, just in itself, however difficult it is

> to check winds, waves, and the inroads
> of vermin and of beasts
>
> a middle term, as it were,
> between gods and men

(It is *Apollonius speaking*, for the first time, after five years)

> And at Babylon
> I was not satisfied with the four golden eggs
> hanging from the roof of the Magi's hall
> which they said, were the tongues of gods
> and were wheels with wings, or spheres,
> vaguely associated with fate

Tyana takes it up: For he
> was not one to settle at all
> for sacred or magic objects in the places of
> that telesma he had his eye on, how
> consecrated a man can make
> himself

Apollonius: How can I find out how
> to be so resistant that
> I make wrong things fly off,
> get off, where they belong,
> which is where nothing is

Tyana: There are no four eggs
> or two, there is no image
> or symbol adequate
> to that which is going on . . .

Apollonius: . . . because I am going on

142

Tyana: It ought to be enough if his action
     is adequate to drive off beasts,
     and all carelessness: the idle only
     are nothing

Apollonius: And it is from them alone that all manipulators
     buy their food: plasma
     of the animal, human or otherwise, and that
        juice
     all witch men, high or low, feed off, the
        white stuff
     —none of it, no superstition, animal or
        magical equals
     the job in hand

Tyana: And how can I teach him
     his hands?

MOVE *three*

For more clue, Apollonius went, this time, West, straight into the Mediterranean world. The dance, and the dancer, now really *travel*. The movement, and the coming of the colors, are much freer, for with the sheaf of his mind and body bound, Apollonius is more open, welcomes place and persons more than his previous preparations allowed for. He is less priggish, intense in another way, without necessity of argument, and with much more excitement to variants, all variations, of countries and of peoples. He takes on the known world, with no nervousness, and with a first assurance that he has a warm mind, however sharp it is, that the heart and the mind are not enemies, are, instead, twins (as the legs are), that motion depends on their functioning together. So he is in no danger (as his world was) of any superstition: he is on the lookout for man, and he is already this side of Caesarism or Christism, has found out that either of these dividings falls into ugly halves—of materialism or immortalism. He knows, as he moves through Alexandria, Athens, Rome, Cadiz, that *his* job, at least, is to find out how to inform all people how best they can stick to the instant, which is both temporal and intense, which is both shape and law.

But one thing he does not know—the words and acts to pass to people so that they may instantly recognize how to avoid both Caesarism and Christism. In lieu of yet knowing a methodology, he looks for it —he looks into everything, politics, art, whore-houses, churches, stores, people sitting in the square at evening, lovers, marriages, idiots, emperors, ravening birds as well as blowflies, eating flowers, seamen, great ladies, beaches where only mangrove precedes him, but always cities, and men thick and single, always, where men are, where they are making ports or new principal streets, how they get crops in to the metropolises, how rich and poor farmers are, how well or not well painters paint, how bad drama is now that there is no Sophocles (who, as he himself is faithful, had been faithful to the doctrines of the healer, Aesculapius). For in a strange way drama is the objectification which has died out of his world and which (in some way he is not yet clear about) is joined to the very objectification (on all other planes of action) which he is so very sure is called for, what he is after, in order to enable man to assert his native harmonics, if man is to be based, once again, wherever he is, on force and dignity.

It is the center of the dance-play, this *dance of the world*, this move across all the Mediterranean, and it is to be imagined, by the dancer, in this way: the world of the 1st century A.D. which Apollonius moves through is already the dispersed thing the West has been since, and through it wanders this other kind of man who somehow or other is not satisfied that the progress, the pushing out, the activity (of Rome pushing into Europe, or Cadiz pushing into the Atlantic), all the expanding of the earth or the heavens (even into Heaven) is worth a thing, is worth a penny more than what he had already, at 20, turned over to his brother.

Yet Apollonius does not know what, for certain, the Naked is which he feels himself turning on, and so, because he does not know, he holds tenaciously to what's before him, to what's in front of his eyes, or in the reach of his hands. And he is almost foolishly "local," heavy with particulars, to the point of seeming a busy-body, a gossip, a flatterer, he is after things so. They laugh at him, that he is so little interested in their pother over power, however much he is interested in them—they feel that, and that he is more interested in them as men, as persons, than anyone else is.

It can be put this way, the dance, to key it: it is a wide investigation into the local, the occasional, what you might even call the ceremonial, but without, on Apollonius' part, any assurance that he knows how to make objects firm, or how firm he is. He is troubled, to cause objects to stay in place, to see clearly his place (the complicating factor of the opposite will at work around him is devilish to keep clear of, to stay clear about). The problem is, how to extricate what he wants from the mess he is surrounded by, how to manage to locate what he himself feels: that life as spirit is in the thing, in the instant, in this man. And then to fix it, in such a way that no one can see him act or hear him talk without, from that illumination, knowing how rich their own life is, and without necessary reference to, any distracting contraries (which in any case—he is sure of that—go on and on).

In his trouble, in his anger, and in his certainty, *Apollonius cries out*:

The whole earth is mine, to journey through it—
as is my life. Look, how handsome it is, how lovely
the tongue is, behind the jumping teeth!
Otherwise,
what is left you, but to shut yourselves up at home
like fattening birds, and gorge your bellies in the dark,
until you burst, with fat?

145

A DANCE OF PASSAGE, before *MOVE four*

He backs up on himself: from Cadiz he comes back through the long Mediterranean to Tyana. He is doing what Odysseus did before him, when he came away from Calypso's Island. But in the interim of those 1000 years, the Mediterranean has grown more self-conscious and so, more confusing—more people, but less wise a place, perhaps. In any event, Apollonius moves backward on a deeper plane of conjecture than the curiosity which marked his coming into the Mediterranean. It is not so much that he has lost any of the curiosity (the more intense a man is, the more curious he is, but the more curious, the more the curiosity is inside, is less obvious, looks masked, even sometimes looks like diffidence). In Apollonius' case, the difficulty of figuring out how to get across what is now the full content of his person is so presented to him—he is so confronted—that he moves differently. The lighting (the colors) can help here if they are changed by graying from the primary, or "map" tones. Or by some massing of them. For the real bother—the new thing Apollonius knows—is quantity: he now understands (what it has been so long necessary to understand) that the quantitative increase of the number of men, of the number of goods, of the known earth is not merely more of same but amounts to—when it gets too large—a qualitative change, unless the vision of man, by admitting this shift of base quantity involves, restates itself to offset the loss. What Apollonius saw, by covering the known world—by hanging from the First Bridge at Byzantium (what was to be Constantinople), by watching the sea traffic at Alexandria (as you now watch it at Manhattan), by prowling the streets of Rome—was that two ills were coming on man: (1) unity was crowding out diversity (man was getting too multiplied to stay clear by way of the old vision of himself, the humanist one, was getting too distracted to abide in his own knowing with any of his old confidence); and (2) unity as a goal (making Rome an empire, say) had, as its intellectual pole an equally mischievous concept, that of the universal—of the "universals" as Socrates and Christ equally had laid them down. Form (which, from the first cities, had stuck by the glue of content to particulars) was suddenly swollen, was being taken as a thing larger a thing outside a thing above any particular, even any given man. And the whole business squatted on Apollonius as a wrong, somehow. He felt in himself that the very notion of goal was false, that to assume that there was any way that end could be separated from instant (from any person or object as any more than the exact striking of that person or object directly and presently on you or me) was as threatening an attack on the roots of life (as a man is life) as was the sucking up into itself by Rome of the function of distribution. Yet he had no answer—yet. He merely had the stubborn sense, with no false arrogation, that he and Tyana were bound together and that that binding was an image of health in the world. He had earlier found that his body and his mind could not be conceived as separable from each other. Now he took it that man and his world too were a sheaf at the harvest, just as seed and the earth were blackly joined in the growing.

So his return to Tyana, this time, is the major one. He has been out, and he comes back with none of the swift illumination (it was an easier part) he had brought back from Bagdad and from Antioch. He is now 40 years old, and at last aware of the dimension of his job: how to offer man a correction which will restore (1) point by point sharpness; and (2) what he knows makes such sharpness— the allaying of any doubt in a man that he belongs, the restoration to him of the sense that everything belongs to him to the degree that he makes himself responsible for it as well as for himself. And Tyana, as his given, as a first fact (no more than that, but no less) looms for him, at this juncture, as in some way intimately connected with the job.

So there is a dance of passage here, a touching before Apollonius once more goes on—for the last time. As he comes back now (as he is pulled back) Tyana expresses the urgency (recognizes it) by rising for the first time, and in the very slowest large movements (no more than great turnings in place) greets him. The actor of Tyana should turn as a stem or trunk might be imagined to turn from the coursings of itself, not at all human but most animate. The danger is, to keep all human, or bough reference out of the arms (any feeling of embrace). Tyana here, in contrast to their movement together on the floor at the beginning of the play, should not touch or look at Apollonius, or let her arms have any overt part in her relevance to him. What we should see, suddenly, is Tyana's change—that Tyana has been changed by Apollonius' actions away from her: it is he, his demand on himself and on life, that has made his birthplace capable of verticality (his wish was, always, to be known as "The Tyanean" and to be called "Apollonius of Tyana"). Verticality, anyway, is the proper way a human body can indicate penetration downward (not by lying down, or crawling around on the ground, as so many do, who do not understand): dignity, after all, is as much a sinking of the feet into the earth as it is containment of the round of the self. And Tyana's turning should have this quality of legs in the earth, and none of the nonsense of clay, or return to dust, or of roots as black and wet and gross. Just black. (It is necessary to emphasize these things because dance, except as one or two are practicing it—who understand that it is not mimesis but kinesis which is its base—is altogether too descriptive and so is—of all things for dance to be!—non-active.)

Apollonius, for his part, also dances without eyes for Tyana. He dances around her, the two being joined together rather by the tensions established between them structurally than by any references (psychological or literary) to each other. They both are properly blind, non-descriptive and at the same time non-mystical: there is no search in this thing (it is better if the actors think of themselves as electronic, as magnet and field, solely, so that they may act out the working out of the function, conjecture). For they both have the same thing on their minds: how Apollonius can get down, get rid of all upstairs, even the finest, even the flights of his mind, even the lyricism (the Beautiful Thing) of his body.

Let Tyana be stem, huge turning solid, and let him be finding out how to be likewise, but as a human being is stem (as place never is). His arms assert multiple planes, the multiple horizontals the vertical makes possible, and his legs the multiple vertical struts, so that, together, these two, make a dance of the sphere of subject and object which Apollonius now has the vision of—as the only full vision capable of delivering man from his split.

As the dance ends, Tyana should go down, and Apollonius himself replace her as the center—for she has enabled him to understand, that what he has not done, with all his concentration, is to commit himself.

MOVE *four*

In this new confidence, Apollonius goes off from Tyana along upper stage left, that is, East, straight East. He should move in larger strides than he has yet used, and the colors of Persia, Afghanistan, and India should come on much more rapidly than did the colors of the other countries, more rapidly and more thickly, perhaps, if that is possible.

INDIA, which he moves to, should be almost an immediately recognizable place to him, in that quick way any of us seize the thing which is right for us, the thing which has been sitting inside us and waiting, suddenly, for its objectification. What Apollonius found there was what he knew: that here was a will which asserted itself inward, a sort of will the West had lost the law of, and so, only turned it outward.

And when Apollonius was asked, later, in Egypt, by the priests—the same priests from whom Herodotus took up,

from whom Plato got his myths, and Pythagoras admitted he learned the secret of secrecy—when they asked Apollonius "Who is wise enough to reform the religion of the Egyptians," he answered, "Any sage who comes from India."
And what he said he saw in India was what he learned there:
"men dwelling
on the earth, and yet not slaves of it, but lovers; I saw them defended on all sides and yet without any defence, I saw men possessed of nothing but what all possess."

And so the dance of India is *a dance of recognition.* St. Augustine said of his experience of recognition, "It was a conflagration of myself," but with Apollonius the terms stay physical in another way, and in that way are neither light nor fire—with him it is a burning, surely, but with nothing consumed, on the contrary, it is as the action of the sun on us and on things, increase is the issue, more growth, more life, more life, leaves, men.

It is from his visit to India that Apollonius' only known personal rite dates: his habit was to separate himself from others three times in a day, at dawn, at noon, and at sundown, to pay his respects, those times, to the sun, to source.

I see no reason why, just here, the dancer should not show, in his movements, exactly that sort of increase of his powers which Classic Indian dance offers any Western dancer—that in no better way can he indicate the sudden power Apollonius takes up than to use such things as (1) a new ability to move by the pulling of the toes alone; (2) by the directioning of the eyes (those night-trained eyes of an Indian dancer which, like a juggler's hands, can keep attention where he pleases); (3) the turkey-neck freeing of the head from the shoulders; and (4) that sinuosity an Indian dancer gets into his arms, so that they move from the bottom of the spine, and are as wings are simultaneously as they are as snakes.

II

The Apollonius who leaves India does not return to Tyana. He does not need to. He is now as fully empowered as man can be, and to the degree that he is so, the dance play shifts: all is now not the action of his shaping himself but he shaping others. He brings his vision to bear in two ways: (1) he wars against Caesarism (and the "universals" which lead to it and which it promotes) by working every way to affect and change emperors and kings, all ruling forces; and (2) he strikes at unity (and the immortalism he takes it such doctrine leads to) by teaching men everywhere, that what is native to themselves, even the places, heroes, and gods local to their neighborhoods, is worth all the state or world religions they are being offered on every hand. And the clue to both attacks is his prime conviction, that *no man should impose his mode of life on others.* (In advising the Indian rajah Phraotes to avoid proselytizing, Apollonius' argument was, it would estrange the rajah too much from his subjects, and when Vespasian asked him how to be a good emperor, Apollonius answered, "In what concerns yourself, act as a private man; in what concerns the state, act likewise." And so he warned Vespasian to beware of taxes and of executions—"Do not lop off," he said, "the ears of corn which show beyond the rest.")

The dance problem is now great. This very code of Apollonius is contrary to drama as we have known it, in which the events are will, are interference with others, are imposings, either of the hero or on the hero or heroine. Here, in these final actions of Apollonius, the reverse is true, it is another sort of will and another sort of action, is drama as Noh is, as the Odyssey was and all the like single actor drama before it reaching back to the Sumerian *epos.* So there is a new sort of learning involved here, and I shall try to aid the dancer by increasing the concreteness of the "situations," by documenting the two ways Apollonius acts, and leave to the dancer what, of the story, he shall use.

A DANCE OF PASSAGE, before MOVE *five*

The first dance after India, however, offers both a climax to what has preceded it as well as an entrance to what follows. For in Egypt, where Apollonius goes directly, on the Upper Nile he finds a community of men who call themselves the GUMNOI, or, THE NAKEDS. It is just such a "fix" as he is after—in the West, in the very area he wants to fight generalization, a huge city of people (like a pueblo in its rudeness—or like Yenan was) who are living together (men, women and children: none of that celibacy) for purposes of commitment, to allow themselves time and place for what they take it life is, preoccupation with itself. (It is this end which has led them, independent of him, to call themselves, the NAKEDS.) At the same time, there is no arbitrary separation from life's details, its daily mechanisms, nor is there any arrogation of race or any excluding: Apollonius finds that the people themselves are a mix of generations of Egyptians, Arabs and Ethiopians, and that they live together without public conflict. They maintain the private principle by assigning, to each family, its own *hiera*, or cell.

All Apollonius does, all the dancer needs to do, is to dance a sort of happiness, a "Naked" happiness, non-interference with others, not so much ecstatic as we know ecstatic, but what ecstatic is, the discipline and joy of anyone when he or she has come to see that compulsion is no good, that nothing is so good as each allowed to be himself alone in the midst of the phenomenal world raging and yet apart. Apollonius dances in such joy, for these NAKEDS have taken up direct from energy where he believes it is, a part of the *daimonos* (which is also become a false word, but it is what Apollonius told his friend, the Roman consul Tellesinus, he knew wisdom to be, "The recognition of the daemonial nature in anything, including ourselves, and only these guileless paths give health").

All that Apollonius does, beyond enjoying these people (he stayed ten years with them, and one of his chief followers, Nilus, came from them) is to do, for the first time here, what he does from then on throughout the ancient world. Let me put it there.

MOVE *five* is two dances, the two acts, Part I THE RESTO-RATION OF THE LOCAL and Part II THE REMINDER TO THE EMPEROR HE IS PRIVATE MAN

Part I is a continuation directly out of the end of the NAKEDS dance, and the dancer should make a progression out of it from Egypt by way of Paphos, Pergamus, Troy and Eleusis (the documentation is below) to Rome (where Part II takes place, also documented below). I suggest this because, whatever the differences of Apollonius' local actions, the dance itself is essentially one dance: in each instance Apollonius' assumption is that any image around which any people concentrate and commit themselves is a usable one just because it is theirs, that truth is never more than its own action, and that all that ever needs attention is the quality of the action.

Apollonius should dance throughout *to* the audience (as he has not had reason to, before, all previous movement, to whatever degree, being discovery of or the involvement of, himself). But now he can, and at Paphos the audience is the priests, at Pergamus his own old teachers, at Troy Achilles, and at Eleusis the Athenians, worshippers of Demeter and Persephone.

Documentation for Part I
   (1) *Paphos:* the worship of Aphrodite—she is represented by a stone symbol the size of a human being and shaped like a pine cone, only smooth; the chief ritual is the tending of a flame of fire (*ancient phallic worship intact*)
   (2) *Pergamus:* the new center of Aesculapian-Pythagorean doctrines—"healing," and chiefly by the prescriptive use of dreams (*ancient physio-psychic curing intact*)

(3) *Troy:* the tomb of Achilles. The story goes, Apollonius spent a night there, and in a dream was told by Achilles that the cult of Palamedes (who is said to have been the Greek who completed the alphabet as Kadmos the Phoenician brought it to Greece, and thus a culture-hero of first importance) needed repair. Achilles told Apollonius where to find the grave in Thessaly, and Apollonius did find it, and did arouse the Thessalians to restore the old accustomed rites to the hero.

(ancient culture-hero rites restored)

(4) *Eleusis:* the temple to Demeter & Persephone— Apollonius was admitted to the rites, and is said, from his special knowledge of chthonic rites elsewhere (Delphi, Dodona, the cave of Trophonius, and in Asia generally) to have increased the priests' understanding of the animal fetishism of the worship (both the pig & the snake) and the significance of the underground "marriage"

(ancient chthonic, & mother-daughter rites)

Note: The mark of all of Apollonius' actions in Ionia and Greece is his care to slight the Olympian gods in favor of the older and more local heroes and divinities. At the same time there are notable rejections by him of all grossness: he refused to visit the labyrinth of the Bull-God of Crete, at Athens he spoke against effeminacy of the Bacchanalia and against the barbarities of gladiatorial combats, and writing to the priests at Delphi against blood-sacrifice, he said, "Heraclitus was a sage, but even he, and 660 years ago at that, never advised the people of Ephesus (whom he took for mud even though they were his kinsmen) to wash out mud with mud!"

MOVE *five*, Part II, THE DANCE OF, AND AGAINST, RULERS

It is one of the remarkable things about Apollonius, how kings, and the Roman emperors, were beholden to him, how much, actually, in the last third of his life, he was

Confucian about such things as his responsibility for the body politic. His influence was enormous, and Vespasian, writing his last letter to his son Titus, reminds him, "We two emperors are solely what we are owing to the good advice of Apollonius." Nerva, too, used him, but Nero and Domitian were his enemies and in both these cases Apollonius had to risk his neck to keep at his work among people. Nero forbade him Rome in 66 A.D. (it was then that Apollonius went to Cadiz) but before he left, when he was being questioned by Nero's agents, he warded off one dangerous thrust. One of the questioners tried to trap him by asking, "What do you think of Nero?" And he answered: "I think better of him than you do, for you think he ought to sing, and I think he ought to keep silent."

When Domitian actually put him on trial, all Apollonius' friends urged him to flee, that his chance to escape death was small. His answer was, that there is always "the moment that suits wisdom best to give death battle," and this seemed to be it, and he gave it. He was acquitted, and there is no better way to give the dancer a sense of the dimension of his subject, in such a situation, than to give Apollonius' reasonings on why he stood up to Domitian:

> The law obliges us to die for liberty, and nature ordains that we should die for our parents, our friends, or our children. All men are bound by these duties.
>
> But a higher duty is laid upon the sage. He must die for his principles and the truth he holds dearer than life. It is not law that lays this choice upon him, it is not nature. It is the strength and courage of his own soul. Though all threaten him, he will not give away nor shall force force from him the slightest falsehood. He will guard the secrets of others' lives and all that has been trusted to his honor as religiously as the secrets of initiation. And I know more than other men, for I know that of all that I know, I know some things for the good, some for the wise, some for myself, some for the Gods, but none for tyrants.

Again, I think that a wise man does nothing alone or by himself: no thought of his is so secret, for he has himself as witness to it. And whether the famous saying "know thyself" be from Apollo or from some sage who learnt to know himself and proclaimed it as a good for all, I think the wise man who knows himself and has his own spirit in constant comradeship, to fight at his right hand, will neither cringe at what the vulgar fear nor dare to do what most men do without the slightest shame.

So long as Domitian ruled (81-96 A.D.) Apollonius kept up his attacks on him. He was visiting Ionia when Domitian was murdered, was at Ephesus, actually, and was speaking at a small park in a suburb of that city at the time murder was taking place in Rome (as was found out afterwards). It was midday, and just then Apollonius broke off, troubled, took three or four steps forward, and definitely out of context cried out, "Strike the tyrant, strike."

THE DISAPPEARANCE, or end of the play

It is here, just here at Ephesus, death of Domitian, date 96 A.D., that Apollonius disappears. And it has usually been left as a sort of proper ending to a holy man's life. But I want this dance to read back into the record just what happened. He had done his work. He was near home. And with pride and ease, let the dancer go back to Tyana, let him come in slow to her as she sits as she sat at the beginning of the play, and let him come down to her, go forward into her arms, and as the lights go down, the color over the whole stage area (the known world) should first go off, color by color, and then, when the same stick of light with which the play opens is all that picks out the two of them, let that light go down, showing us the two of them as they were, but with this one difference, that, now Apollonius's back is to the audience, and they shape together an ambiguous, double backed thing as darkness returns and is final.

IV

The lines which hook-over should be read
as though they lay out right and flat to the
horizon or Eternity.

Note by Charles Olson
for this book, 1966.

THE K

Take, then, my answer:
there is a tide in a man
moves him to his moon and,
though it drop him back
he works through ebb to mount
the run again and swell
to be tumescent I

The affairs of men remain a chief concern

We have come full circle.
I shall not see the year 2000
unless I stem straight from my father's mother,
break the fatal male small span.
If that is what the tarot pack proposed
I shall hang out some second story window
and sing, as she, one unheard liturgy

Assume I shall not.
Is it of such concern when what shall be
already is within the moonward sea?

Full circle: an end to romans, hippocrats and christians.
There! is a tide in the affairs of men to discern

Shallows and miseries shadows from the cross,
ecco men and dull copernican sun.
Our attention is simpler
The salts and minerals of the earth return
The night has a love for throwing its shadows around a man
a bridge, a horse, the gun, a grave.

LA PRÉFACE

The dead in via
        in vita nuova
              in the way
You shall lament who know they are as tender as the horse is.
You, do not you speak who know not.

      "I will die about April 1st . . ." going off
      "I weigh, I think, 80 lbs . . ." scratch
      "My name is NO RACE" address
      Buchenwald new Altamira cave
      With a nail they drew the object of the hunt.

Put war away with time, come into space.
It was May, precise date, 1940. I had air my lungs could breathe.
He talked, via stones　a stick　sea rock　a hand of earth.
It is now, precise, repeat. I talk of Bigmans organs
he, look, the lines! are polytopes.
And among the DPS—deathhead
              at the apex
                   of the pyramid.

Birth in the house is the One of Sticks, cunnus in the crotch.
Draw it thus: (　) 1910 (
It is not obscure. We are the new born, and there are no flowers.
Document means there are no flowers
              and no parenthesis.

It is the radical, the root, he and I, two bodies
We put our hands to these dead.

The closed parenthesis reads: the dead bury the dead,
    and it is not very interesting.
Open, the figure stands at the door, horror his
and gone, possessed, o new Osiris, Odysseus ship.
He put the body there as well as they did whom he killed.

Mark that arm. It is no longer gun.
We are born not of the buried but these unburied dead
crossed stick, wire-led, Blake Underground

The Babe
            the Howling Babe

THE MOEBIUS STRIP

Upon a Moebius strip
materials and the weights of pain
their harmony

A man within himself upon an empty ground.
His head lay heavy on a huge right hand
itself a leopard on
his left and angled shoulder.
His back a stave, his side a hole into the bosom of a sphere.

His head passed down a sky (as suns the circle of a year).
His other shoulder, open side and thigh maintained,
by law of conservation of
the graveness of his center,
their clockwise fall.
Then he knew, so came to apogee
and earned and wore himself as amulet.

I saw another man lift up a woman in his arms
he helmeted, she naked too, protected as Lucrece by her alarms.
Her weight tore down his right and muscled thigh
but they in turn returned upon the left
to carry violence outcome in her eye.
It was his shoulder that sustained, the right,
bunched as by buttocks or by breasts,
and gave them back the leisure of their rape.

And three or four who danced,
so joined as triple-thighed and bowed and arrowed folk
who spilled their pleasure once as yoke

on stone-henge plain.
Their bare and lovely bodies sweep, in round
of viscera, of legs
of turned-out hips and glance, bound
each to other, nested eggs
of elements in trance.

THE RING OF

it was the west wind caught her up, as
she rose
from the genital
wave, and bore her from the delicate
foam, home
to her isle

and those lovers
of the difficult, the hours
of the golden day welcomed her, clad her, were
as though they had made her, were wild
to bring this new thing born
of the ring of the sea pink
& naked, this girl, brought her
to the face of the gods, violets
in her hair

Beauty, and she
said no to zeus & them all, all were not or
was it she chose the ugliest
to bed with, or was it straight
and to expiate the nature of beauty, was it?

knowing hours, anyway,
she did not stay long, or the lame
was only one part, & the handsome
mars had her   And the child
had that name, the arrow of
as the flight of, the move of
his mother who adorneth

with myrtle the dolphin and words
they rise, they do who
are born of like
elements

MERCE OF EGYPT

1

I sing the tree is a heron
I praise long grass.
I wear the lion skin
over the long skirt
to the ankle. The ankle
is a heron

I look straightly backward. Or I bend to the side straightly
to raise the sheaf
up the stick of the leg
as the bittern's leg, raised
as slow as
his neck grows
as the wheat. The presentation,
the representation,
is flat

I am followed by women and a small
                         boy in white carrying a duck,
all have flat feet and, foot before foot,
                      the women with black wigs
And I intent
upon idlers,
and flowers

2

          the sedge
as tall as I am, the rushes
as I am

      as far as I am animal, antelope
with such's attendant carnivores

                                        and rows of beaters
drive the game to the hunter, or into nets,
where it is thick-wooded or there are open spaces
with low shrubs

3

I speak downfall, the ball of my foot
on the neck of the earth, the hardsong
of the rise of all trees, the jay
who uses the air. I am the recovered sickle
with the grass-stains still on the flint of its teeth.
I am the six-rowed barley
they cut down.

I am tree. The boy of the back of my legs
is roots. I am water fowl
when motion is the season of my river, and the wild boar
casts me. But my time
is hawkweed,

4

I hold what the wind blows, and silt.
I hide in the swamps of the valley to escape civil war,
and marauding soldiers. In the new procession
I am first, and carry wine
made of dandelions. The new rites
are my bones

I built my first settlement
in groves

5

                as they would flail crops
when the spring comes, and flood, the tassels
rise, as my head

THE KINGFISHERS

1

What does not change / is the will to change

He woke, fully clothed, in his bed. He
remembered only one thing, the birds, how
when he came in, he had gone around the rooms
and got them back in their cage, the green one first,
she with the bad leg, and then the blue,
the one they had hoped was a male

Otherwise? Yes, Fernand, who had talked
lispingly of Albers & Angkor Vat.
He had left the party without a word.
How he got up, got into his coat,
I do not know. When I saw him, he was
at the door, but it did not matter,
he was already sliding along the wall of the night, losing himself
in some crack of the ruins. That it should have
been he who said, "The kingfishers!
who cares
for their feathers
now?"

His last words had been, "The pool is slime." Suddenly everyone,
ceasing their talk, sat in a row around him, watched
they did not so much hear, or pay attention, they
wondered, looked at each other, smirked, but listened,
he repeated and repeated, could not go beyond his thought
"The pool   the kingfishers' feathers were wealth   why
did the export stop?"

It was then he left

2

I thought of the E on the stone, and of what Mao said
la lumiere"
> but the kingfisher

de l'aurore"
> but the kingfisher flew west

est devant nous!
> he got the color of his breast
> from the heat of the setting sun!

The features are, the feebleness of the feet
> > (syndactylism of the 3rd & 4th digit)

the bill, serrated, sometimes a pronounced beak, the wings
where the color is, short and round, the tail
inconspicuous.

But not these things were the factors. Not the birds.
The legends are
legends. Dead, hung up indoors, the kingfisher
will not indicate a favoring wind,
or avert the thunderbolt. Nor, by its nesting,
still the waters, with the new year, for seven days.
It is true, it does nest with the opening
> > year, but not on the waters.

It nests at the end of a tunnel bored by itself in a bank. There,
six or eight white and translucent eggs are laid, on fishbones
not on bare clay, on bones thrown up in pellets by the birds.

> On these rejectamenta

(as they accumulate they form a cup-shaped
> > structure) the young are born.

And, as they are fed and grow, this
> nest of excrement and decayed fish becomes
> a dripping, fetid mass

Mao concluded:
> nous devons
> > nous lever
> > > et agir!

3

When the attentions change / the jungle
leaps in
          even the stones are split
                      they rive
Or,
enter
that other conqueror we more naturally recognize
he so resembles ourselves

But the E
cut so rudely on that oldest stone
sounded otherwise,
was differently heard

as, in another time, were treasures used:

(and, later, much later, a fine ear thought
a scarlet coat)

          "of green feathers   feet, beaks and eyes
          of gold

          "animals likewise,
          resembling snails

          "a large wheel, gold,
                      with figures of unknown four-foots,
          and worked with tufts of leaves, weight
          3800 ounces

          "last, two birds, of thread and featherwork, the quills
          gold, the feet
          gold, the two birds perched on two reeds
          gold, the reeds arising from two embroidered mounds,
          one yellow, the other
          white.

"And from each reed hung
seven feathered tassels.

In this instance, the priests
(in dark cotton robes, and dirty,
their dishevelled hair matted with blood, and flowing wildly
over their shoulders)
rush in among the people, calling on them
to protect their gods

And all now is war
where so lately there was peace,
and the sweet brotherhood, the use
of tilled fields.

4

Not one death but many,
not accumulation but change, the feed-back proves,
                                                    the feed-back is
the law

          Into the same river no man steps twice
          When fire dies air dies
          No one remains, nor is, one

Around an appearance, one common model, we grow up
many. Else how is it,
if we remain the same,
we take pleasure now
in what we did not take pleasure before? love
contrary objects? admire and / or find fault? use
other words, feel other passions, have
nor figure, appearance, disposition, tissue
the same?

          To be in different states without a change
          is not a possibility

We can be precise. The factors are
in the animal and / or the machine the factors are
communication and / or control, both involve
the message. And what is the message? The message is
a discrete or continuous sequence of measurable
                                        events distributed in time

is the birth of air, is
the birth of water, is
a state between
the origin and
the end, between
birth and the beginning of
another fetid nest

is change, presents
no more than itself

And the too strong grasping of it,
when it is pressed together and condensed,
loses it

This very thing you are

                              II

        They buried their dead in a sitting posture
        serpent   cane   razor   ray of the sun

        And she sprinkled water on the head of the child, crying
        "Cioa-coatl! Cioa-coatl!"
        with her face to the west

        Where the bones are found, in each personal heap
        with what each enjoyed, there is always
        the Mongolian louse

The light is in the east. Yes. And we must rise, act. Yet
in the west, despite the apparent darkness (the whiteness
which covers all), if you look, if you can bear, if you can,
                                                    long enough

            as long as it was necessary for him, my guide
            to look into the yellow of that longest-lasting rose

so you must, and, in that whiteness, into that face,
                                    with what candor, look

and, considering the dryness of the place
        the long absence of an adequate race

            (of the two who first came, each a conquistador,
                                one healed, the other
            tore the eastern idols down, toppled
            the temple walls, which, says the excuser
            were black from human gore)

hear
hear, where the dry blood talks
        where the old appetite walks

                            la piu saporita et migliore
                            che si possa truovar al mondo

where it hides, look
in the eye how it runs
in the flesh / chalk

            but under these petals
            in the emptiness
            regard the light, contemplate
            the flower

whence it arose

172

with what violence benevolence is bought
what cost in gesture justice brings
what wrongs domestic rights involve
what stalks
this silence

what pudor pejorocracy affronts
how awe, night-rest and neighborhood can rot
what breeds where dirtiness is law
what crawls
below

III

I am no Greek, hath not th'advantage.
And of course, no Roman:
he can take no risk that matters,
the risk of beauty least of all.

But I have my kin, if for no other reason than
(as he said, next of kin) I commit myself, and,
given my freedom, I'd be a cad
if I didn't. Which is most true.

It works out this way, despite the disadvantage.
I offer, in explanation, a quote:
si j'ai du goût, ce n'est guères
que pour la terre et les pierres

Despite the discrepancy (an ocean   courage   age)
this is also true: if I have any taste
it is only because I have interested myself
in what was slain in the sun

I pose you your question:

shall you uncover honey / where maggots are?

I hunt among stones

THE PRAISES

She who was burned more than half her body
$$\text{skipped out of death}$$

Observing
that there are five solid figures, the Master
(or so Aetius reports, in the *Placita*)
concluded that
the Sphere of the Universe arose from
the dodecahedron

> whence Alexander,
> appearing in a dream to Antiochus,
> showed him
> And on the morrow, the enemy (the Galates)
> ran before it,
> before the sign, that is

1

By Filius Bonacci, his series, rediscovered Pisa 1202,
$$\text{we shall attack,}$$
for it, too, proceeds asymptotically toward the graphic
$$\text{and tangible, the law}$$
now determined to be
phi

> its capital role in the distribution of
> leaves   seeds   branches on a stem (ex.,
> the ripe sun-flower)
>
> the ratios ⅝, ⅘₁₃
> in the seed-cones of fir-trees,

the ratio $2\frac{1}{34}$
in normal daisies

Pendactylism is general in the animal kingdom.
But crystals . . . there, pentagonal forms or lattices
do not, can not appear

So we have it: star and jelly fish, the sea urchin.
And because there is an ideal and constant angle which,
for leaves and branches on a stem, produces
the maximum exposition to light, that light vertical,
fruit blossoms   the briar rose   the passion flower
But lilies   tulips   the hyacinth, like crystals . . .

Here we must stop   And ponder   For nature,
though she is, as you know (so far, that is
as it is allowed to a mortal to know) from all
                                        points of view
similar to herself, yet minerals . . .

          o, that's not fair, let
          woman keep her jewels, odd man
          his pleasure of her glow, let
          your lady Nephritite
          pumice her malachite, paint
          her lids green against the light

Sd he:
          to dream takes no effort
             to think is easy
                to act is more difficult
          but for a man to act after he has taken thought, this!
          is the most difficult thing of all

2

We turn now to Ammonius,
who was present when Nero was,

who is full of delights,
& who smiles quickly

    the epiphanies, he says, in this case are four:
    1st, to such as begin to learn & to inquire,
    the Pythian response,
    with flute

    (2) when part of the truth is glimpsed, the sun
    (a creature of four-fold eyes and heads,
    of a ram a bull a snake the bright-eyed lion)
    This is little, even though the drum
    is added

    When a person has got the knowledge, Ammonius
    (and he does not mean to be ambiguous)
    confers one overwhelming title:
    he says a man may then call himself
                     OF THEBES. He may sing

    The last, and triumphant mode, I leave, as he leaves it,
    untranslated: when men are active, enjoy thought,
                        that is to say
    when they talk, they are LESKENOI. They rage

Which is why what is related must remain enigmatic
And why Ammonius excepts, from these epiphanies,
those who are entirely brutish.

Which brings us to what concerns us in the present inquiry.

    Avert, avert, avoid
    pollution, to be clean
    in a dirty time

        O Wheel, aid us
        to get the gurry off

You would have a sign. Look:
to fly? a fly can do that;
to try the moon? a moth
as well; to walk on water? a straw
precedes you

        O Wheel! draw
        that truth
        to my house

Like pa does, not like sis,
on all detractors, piss, o advertised earth!
And you, o lady Moon, observe my love,
whence it arose

Whence it arose,
and who it is who sits,
there at the base of the skull, locked
in his throne of bone, that mere pea of bone
where the axes meet, cross-roads of the system
god, converter, discloser, he will answer,
will look out, if you will look, look!

3

What has been lost
is the secret of secrecy, is
the value, viz., that the work get done, and quickly,
without the loss of due and profound respect for
the materials

which is not so easy as it sounds, nor
can it permit the dispersion which follows from
too many having too little
knowledge

        Says Iamblichus:
    by shipwreck, he perished (Hippasus, that is)
    the first to publish (write down, divulge)

the secret,
the construction of, from 12 pentagons,
the sphere

"Thus was he punished for his impiety"

What is necessary is
containment,
that that which has been found out by work
                        may, by work be passed on
(without due loss of force)
for use
        USE

"And they took over power, political power,
                        in Gr Greece, including
Sicily, and maintained themselves, even after the Master
                        died, until,
at Metapontum, the mob

"Only Philalaos, and Lysis, did not perish in the fire. Later,
Archytas it was, pupil of Philalaos, who, friend to Plato,
                        initiated him,
and, at Tarentum

4

Which is about what we had to say,
the clues, anyhow

What belongs to art and reason is

                        the knowledge of

                                consequences

L da V, his notebook:

                Every natural action obeys by
                the straightest possible process

THERE WAS A YOUTH
WHOSE NAME WAS
THOMAS GRANGER

1

From the beginning, SIN
and the reason, note, known from the start

says Mr. bradford: As it is with waters when
their streames are stopped or damed up, wickednes
(Morton, Morton, Morton)
here by strict laws as in no place more,
or so much, that I have known or heard of,
and yᵉ same more nerly looked unto
(Tom Granger)
so, as it cannot rune in a comone road of liberty
as it would, and is inclined,
it searches every wher (everywhere)
and breaks out wher it getts vente, says he

Rest, Tom, in your pit where they put you
a great & large pitte digged of purposs for them
of Duxbery, servant, being aboute 16. or 17. years of age
his father & mother living at the time at Sityate

espetially drunkennes & unclainnes
incontinencie betweene persons unmaried
but some maried persons allso
And that which is worse
(things fearfull to name)

HAVE BROAK FORTH OFTENER THAN ONCE
IN THIS LAND

indicted for ye same) with
a mare, a cowe, tow goats, five sheep, 2. calves
and a turkey   (Plymouth Plantation)

Now follows ye ministers answers

3

Mr Charles Channcys   a reverend, godly, very larned man
who shortly thereafter, due to a difference aboute baptising
he holding it ought only to be by diping
that sprinkling was unlawful, removed him selfe
to the same Sityate, a minister to ye church ther

in this case proved, by reference to ye judicials of Moyses
& see: Luther, Calvin, Hen: Bulin:. Theo: Beza. Zanch:
what greevous sin in ye sight of God,
by ye instigation of burning lusts, set on fire of hell,
to proceede to contactum & fricationem ad emissionem seminis,
        &c.,
& y^t contra naturam, or to attempt ye grosse acts of

4

Mr Bradford: I forbear perticulers.
And accordingly he was cast by ye jury,
and condemned.

                It being demanded of him
the youth confessed he had it of another
who had long used it in old England,
and they kept catle togeather.

And after executed about ye 8. of Sept^r, 1642.
A very sade spectakle it was; for first the mare,

and then ye cowe, and ye rest of ye lesser catle,
were kild before his face, according to ye law
Levit: 20.15.

and then he him selfe

and no use made of any part of them

IN COLD HELL, IN THICKET

In cold hell, in thicket, how
abstract (as high mind, as not lust, as love is) how
strong (as strut or wing, as polytope, as things are
constellated) how
strung, how cold
can a man stay (can men) confronted
thus?

All things are made bitter, words even
are made to taste like paper, wars get tossed up
like lead soldiers used to be
(in a child's attic) lined up
to be knocked down, as I am,
by firings from a spit-hardened fort, fronted
as we are, here, from where we must go

God, that man, as his acts must, as there is always
a thing he can do, he can raise himself, he raises
on a reed he raises his

Or, if it is me, what
he has to say

1

What has he to say?
In hell it is not easy
to know the traceries, the markings
(the canals, the pits, the mountings by which space
declares herself, arched, as she is, the sister,

awkward stars drawn for teats to pleasure him, the brother
who lies in stasis under her, at ease as any monarch or
a happy man

How shall he who is not happy, who has been so made unclear,
who is no longer privileged to be at ease, who,
$\qquad\qquad\qquad\qquad\qquad\qquad$ in this brush, stands
reluctant, imageless, unpleasured, caught in a sort of hell, how
shall be convert this underbrush, how turn this unbidden place
how trace and arch again
the necessary goddess?

2

The branches made against the sky are not of use, are
already done, like snow-flakes, do not, cannot service
him who has to raise (Who puts this on, this damning
$\qquad\qquad\qquad\qquad\qquad\qquad$ of his flesh?)
he can, but how far, how sufficiently far can he raise
$\qquad\qquad\qquad\qquad\qquad\qquad$ the thickets of
this wilderness?

$\qquad$ How can he change, his question is
$\qquad$ these black and silvered knivings, these
$\qquad$ awkwardnesses?

$\qquad$ How can he make these blood-points into panels,
$\qquad\qquad\qquad\qquad\qquad\qquad$ into sides
$\qquad\qquad$ for a king's, for his own
$\qquad\qquad$ for a wagon, for a sleigh, for the beak of,
$\qquad\qquad\qquad\qquad\qquad\qquad$ the running sides of
$\qquad$ a vessel fit for
$\qquad$ moving?

$\qquad$ How can he make out, he asks,
$\qquad$ of this low eye-view,
$\qquad$ size?

And archings traced and picked enough to hold
to stay, as she does, as he, the brother, when,
here where the mud is, he is frozen, not daring
where the grass grows, to move his feet from fear
he'll trespass on his own dissolving bones, here
where there is altogether too much remembrance?

3

The question, the fear he raises up himself against
(against the same each act is proffered, under the eyes
each fix, the town of the earth over, is managed) is: Who
am I?

Who am I but by a fix, and another,
a particle, and the congery of particles carefully picked
                                        one by another,

          as in this thicket, each
          smallest branch, plant, fern, root
          —roots lie, on the surface, as nerves are laid open—
          must now (the bitterness of the taste of her) be
          isolated, observed, picked over, measured, raised
          as though a word, an accuracy were a pincer!
                                                  this
               is the abstract, this
               is the cold doing, this
               is the almost impossible

So shall you blame those
who give it up, those who say
it isn't worth the struggle?

                    (Prayer
Or a death as going over to—shot by yr own forces—to
a greener place?

any longer
usable)

By fixes only (not even any more by shamans)
can the traceries
be brought out

II

ya, selva oscura, but hell now
is not exterior, is not to be got out of, is
the coat of your own self, the beasts
emblazoned on you   And who
can turn this total thing, invert
and let the ragged sleeves be seen
by any bitch or common character?   Who
can endure it where it is, where the beasts are met,
where yourself is, your beloved is, where she
who is separate from you, is not separate, is not
goddess, is, as your core is,
the making of one hell

where she moves off, where she is
no longer arch

(this is why he of whom we speak does not move, why
he stands so awkard where he is, why
his feet are held, like some ragged crane's
off the nearest next ground, even from
the beauty of the rotting fern his eye
knows, as he looks down, as,
in utmost pain if cold can be so called,
he looks around his battlefield, this
rotted place where men did die, where boys

and immigrants have fallen, where nature
(the years that she's took over)
does not matter, where

                    that men killed, do kill, that woman kills
                    is part, too, of his question

2

That it is simple, what the difference is—
that a man, men, are now their own wood
and thus their own hell and paradise
that they are, in hell or in happiness, merely
something to be wrought, to be shaped, to be carved, for use, for
others

does not in the least lessen his, this unhappy man's
obscurities, his
confrontations

He shall step, he
will shape, he
is already also
moving off

                    into the soil, on to his own bones

he will cross

                    (there is always a field,
                    for the strong there is always
                    an alternative)

                              But a field
                    is not a choice, is
                    as dangerous as a prayer, as a death, as any
                    misleading, lady

He will cross

> And is bound to enter (as she is)
> a later wilderness.
> > > Yet
> what he does here, what he raises up
> (he must, the stakes are such

> > > > this at least
> is a certainty, this
> is a law, is not one of the questions, this
> is what was talked of as
> —what was it called, demand?)

> He will do what he now does, as she will, do
> carefully, do
> without wavering,
> without
> > as even the branches,
> > even in this dark place, the twigs
> > > > how

> > even the brow
> of what was once to him a beautiful face

> as even the snow-flakes waver in the light's eye

> > as even forever wavers (gutters
> > in the wind of loss)

> > even as he will forever waver

> > precise as hell is, precise
> > as any words, or wagon,
> > can be made

TO GERHARDT, THERE, AMONG EUROPE'S THINGS OF WHICH HE HAS WRITTEN US IN HIS "BRIEF AN CREELEY UND OLSON"

so pawed,
by this long last Bear-son

      with no crockery broken,
      but no smile in my mouth

            June 28th, '51, on this horst
            on the Heat Equator, a mediterranean sea
            to the east, and north
            what saves America from desert, waters
            and thus rain-bearing winds,
            by subsidence, salt-waters
             (by which they came,
             the whelps, looking
             for youth

Which they found.

         And have continuously sought

                      to kill

        (o Old Man,
     in winter, when before me, cross my path

in summer, when behind me, cross my path

If you want to shut yourself in, shut yourself in
If you do not want to shut yourself in, come out

> A zoo
> is what he's come to, the old
> Beginner, the old
> Winner

Who took all,
for awhile

> (My grandfather, my grandmother,
> why have you died?
> Did a hand to hand struggle come?
> Did a war, the size of a man's fist come?)

1

The proposition, Gerhardt
is to get it straight, right
from the start.

> Help raise the bones
> of the great man.
>
> Meat and bones we won't throw away.
> We pile it up in a lonely place.
>
> We do not throw on the ground.
> Your meat and bones without purpose.
> We take bones and meat.
>
> O Grandfather,
> you went to war

The first duty is
to knock out his teeth, saying
"These are the teeth with which you devour all animals."

I offer you no proper names
either from great cities
on the other side of civilization
which have only to be visited
to be got the hell out of, by bus
or motorcycle, simply because place
as a force is a lie.
or at most a small truth,
now that man has no oar to screw down into the earth, and say
here i'll plant, does not know
why he should cease
staying on the prowl

        You climbed up the tree after some foul berry
        and fell down and died
        You ate berries, fell from the rock
        and died
        You ate sorb berries
        and died
        You ate raspberries,
        drowned in the swamp and died

Or from the other side of time, from a time
                    on the other side of yourself
from which you have so lightly borrowed men,
               naming them as though,
like your litany of Europe's places, you could take up
their power: magic, my light-fingered faust,
is not so easily sympathetic. Nor are the ladies
worn so decoratively.

        The top of the spring plant
        noisily chewing

The top of the summer plant
noisily chewing

On a summer day walk before and behind me
on a winter day

2

Nor can I talk of method, in the face of your letter,
in verse or otherwise,
as though it were a dance
of rains, or schmerz, of words as signs worn
like a toupee on the head of a Poe cast
in plaster, any method otherwise than
he practiced it who gave it up,
after a summer in his mother's barn,
because the place smelled so, because time
his time, precisely this now
And with no back references, no
floating over Asia arrogating
how a raiding party moves in advance of a nation thereby
eventually
giving a language the international power
poets take advantage of. As they also,
with much less reason, from too much economics speak
of the dream
in a peasant's bent shoulders, as though it were true
they cared a damn
for his conversation

On a mountain with dry stalks, walk
with a resounding tread

On a mountain with meadow-sweet
walk with a resounding tread

On the way to your fathers,
join them

3

Nor of a film, or of strange birds,
or of ordinary ones. Nor with the power of American vocables
would I arm you in Kansas, when you come,
or there, if you have to stay, where you feel so strongly
the dead center of the top of time

                    I am giving you a present

                    I am giving you a present

For you forget (forgetting
is much more your problem
than you know, right-handed one
who so beautifully reminds me
that the birds stand
in the middle of the air
and that always, in that apsed place
in which so many have kneeled
as I do not have the soul to kneel, the fields
are forever harvested, and happy heaven
leans over backwards
to pour its blessings by downfall
on to black earth

Admitting that among the ruins
        with a like schmerz in every vessel of his throat,
        he repeated, "Among the ruins, among them
        the finest memory in the Orient"
one will go about picking up old pieces
        bric-a-brac, he snorted, who did not know whereof he spoke,
        he had so allowed himself to be removed, to back-trail
or put it immediately out of the mind, as some can,
stuff the construction hole quickly with a skyscraper

but you will remember that even Caesar comes to this,
                                        certainly you

who has written of Hamlet's death, who is able to handle
                              such large counters
as the classic poet handled bank-notes in our time, before prizes
were his lot, and I am envious, who can do neither

that the point of the rotting of man in his place is also
(beside the long-lived earth of good farmers, its manuring,
what Duncan pointed out America and Russia are
                              very careless with)
what blows about and blocks a hole where the wind
                              was used to go

          (While walking on the earth with stalks
          you received a present

          While walking on the earth with the stalks of plants
          your head was crushed

          You could not see, your eyes got small,
          you could not defecate, you were small
          you could not,
          therefore you died

It is a rod of mountain ash I give you, Rainer Maria Gerhardt,
instead of any other thing, in order that you may also be
left-handed, as he was, your Grandfather,
whom you have all forgotten, have even lost the song of, how
he was to be addressed:

          "Great man,
          in climbing up the tree,
          broke his leg."

I am urging you from here
where nothing is brutal,
not even the old economics

(I do not dare to breathe
for what I know the new
will do) and only the kids kill
frigate-birds, because they have to
to develop a throwing arm

        (as your people knew, if I can lead you
        to go back far enough,
        which is not one step from where you are

           "His ear is the earth.
           Let you be careful"

        that he must be hunted, that to eat
        you shall bring him down

           "Your head
           is the size of a ladle

           Your soul
           is of the size of a thread

           Do not enter my soul by day,
           do not enter my dreams by night"

        that woman—who is, with more resistance
        than you seem to have allowed, named—
        lends herself to him as concubine

what you forget is, you

are their son! You are not

Telemachus. And that you come back

under your own

steam

There are no broken stones, no statues, no images,
                                    phrases, composition
otherwise than
what Creeley and I also have,
and without reference to
what reigned in the house
and is now well dismissed

Let you pray to him, we say
who are without such fatherhood:

      "Show your house in spring.

      Show a mound of snow in your house in winter.

      In summer go back of and in front of
      the children.

      Think not badly of the man, go right."

4

Or come here
where we will welcome you
with nothing but what is, with
no useful allusions, with no birds
but those we stone, nothing to eat
but ourselves, no end and no beginning, I assure you, yet
not at all primitive, living as we do in a space
                                    we do not need to contrive

And with predecessors who, though they are
                                    not our nouns, the verbs
are like!

So we are possessed of what you cry over, time
and magic numbers

Language,
my enemie,
is no such system:

"Hey, old man, the war arrived.

Be still, old man.

Your mouth is shut,

your door is shut,"

As I said, I am giving you a present.
To all false dimensions,
including his superb one
who refused to allow the social question in,
to all such fathers and false girls
(one of his, I notice, you take, seriously)
why not say what, somewhere, you must hear the echo of?

"One eye
sees heaven,
another eye
sees earth"

For the problem is one of focus, of the field as well as the point of
vision: you will solve your problem best
without displacement

"One ear
hears heaven,
another ear
hears earth."

In such simplicities I would have you address me,
another time

The old man, my grandfather, died.
The old woman, my grandmother, died.
And now my father visits me, clothed
in a face he never wore, with an odor
I do not know as his, as his was meadow-sweet.
He sits, grieving, that she should have worried,
and I look up at him as he sits there
and if I am his son, this man
is from as far a place and time
as yours is, carries with him
the strangeness you and I will carry
for our sons, and for like reason,
that we are such that can be pawed

"We are no murderers," they used so carefully to say.

"We have put in order the bones of him
    whom others kill."

You see, we are experienced of what you speak of: silence
with no covering of ashes, geraniums also
and loaded with aphis

            of all but war,

but war, too, is dead as the lotus is dead

            And our hardness

has been exaggerated. You see,
we see nothing downward: we walk, as your grandfather walked,
without looking at his feet

            "And because of meeting the great man,
            a feast is held

Warm yourself,
over the fire of grandfather

This is an offering to the guests, a holiday
of the great man

He will feel satisfied

He will not take revenge

The stick is a reminder, Gerhardt. And the song? what seems
to have been forgotten?

Here it is (as we say here, in our anti-cultural speech, made up
of particulars only, which we don't, somehow,
                                        confuse with gossip:

    "To his resting place in spring,

      to his house in autumn,

      I shall go

      With autumn plant, arouse the mountain

      With spring plant, arouse the mountain

      In summer, walk in the background,
      do not frighten the children,
      do not sniff, neither here
      nor there."

ANECDOTES OF THE LATE WAR

1.

the lethargic vs violence as alternatives of each other
                                    for los americanos

    & U S Grant (at Shiloh, as ex.) had the gall to stay
    inside a lethargy until it let him down into either
    vice (Galena, or, as president) or
    a virtue of such a movement as, example,
    Vicksburg

    say that he struck, going down, either
    morass or
    rock—and when it was rock, he was

—this wld seem to be the power in the principle—

able to comprehend the movement of mass of men, the

transposition of the

Mississippi   (Or

continents, example,

somebody else than:

grant

    better, that is, that a man stay lethargic than

blow somebody's face off—off,

the face of, blow

the earth

2.

that (like the man sd) Booth
killing Lincoln is the melodrama right with
the drama: Mister Christ and
Broadway
              Or going out to Bull Run looking for
Waterloo. the
diorama. And having to get the fastidious hell home
that afternoon
as fast as the carriage horses
can't make it (Lee Highway
littered with broken
elegances

              Reverse of
sic transit gloria, the
Latin American whom the cab driver told me
he picked up at Union Station had
one word of english—link-
cone. And drove him
straight to the monument, the man
went up the stairs and fell down on his knees
where he could see the statue and stayed there
in the attitude of prayer

3.

whoop,
went the bird

in the tree the day
the fellow
fell down
in the thicket

whoop, was the bird's
lay as the fellow lay

and I picked up a minie ball
(the way
it can be
again
of an afternoon,

or with the French girl Brandy Station
was
thick grass
and the gray house and back of it

yes   mam   the   movement

of horses, as

—I repeat—

the bird.

4.

West Point it wasn't. Nor New England. Nor
those cavalry
flauntlets
       As the Mexican War was
       filibusterers
       in the West,
       and cadets
       before Chapultepec: the elevator

goink down

from waterloo,

the Civil War

was the basement. Only nobody

except butternut

and his fellow on the other side

wanted to believe it, they all wanted

what Jay Gould got

(and Joe Blow got swap
in the side of the head

5.

Now you take this Forrest, Nathan Bedford Forrest. He stalks
the Western theater of operations as something the English, to
this day, think Lee wouldn't have surpassed had anybody dared
to give this Memphis slave-trader the width of men and field to
command which he only had as first Grand Wizard of the Ku
Klux Klan. And didn't use, Forrest could already avoid the
temptation of the Filibusterer, he had applied first principles
in the War.

What I'd wanted to say was,
that he's a man so locked in the act of himself

    (right up to after Davis had been taken
    and no last movie scene to the way he was still
    cutting tracks behind U. S. Army units, a very

exact and busy man.

I also have to voice this impression of him to give, if it
does, the sense of how he was:

> he's like a man his tongue was cut out,
> before even Shiloh showed him
> an extraordinary executive
> of men horses and goods

6.

Two things still aren't brought in to give context to the War:
(1), that you don't get Grant except as you find what he was
that Geo Washington also comes alive at only if you realize he
was to real estate—

> and I mean land
when land was as oil steel and what, now?

Managing men, wasn't it, when men suddenly what was Grant's

because of the industrial revolution

were what the guys who died then were

> For the first time,
like that, the sprawled fellow Devil's Glen, natural
resource.

> The other half of it—(2)—that each one of them,

Butternut,

and Yankee Doodle,

weren't as different as North and South, farmer and factory etc.

They were—for the first time—enough of them.

                          Plus railroad tracks
                          to be moved around as

utility

      The leaders,   Grant Sherman Forrest not
                        Jeb Stuart
      and themselves

      the birth of

      the recent   And Lincoln

      likewise   (after Christ

      Link-cone

7.

You take it
from there

8.

What he said was, in that instance
I got there first
with the most men

Grant didn't hurry.
He just had the most.

More of the latter died.

AS THE DEAD PREY UPON US

As the dead prey upon us,
they are the dead in ourselves,
awake, my sleeping ones, I cry out to you,
disentangle the nets of being!

I pushed my car, it had been sitting so long unused.
I thought the tires looked as though they only needed air.
But suddenly the huge underbody was above me,
                             and the rear tires
were masses of rubber and thread variously clinging together

as were the dead souls in the living room, gathered
about my mother, some of them taking care to pass
beneath the beam of the movie projector, some record
playing on the victrola, and all of them
desperate with the tawdriness of their life in hell

I turned to the young man on my right and asked, "How is it,
there?" And he begged me protestingly don't ask, we are poor
poor. And the whole room was suddenly posters
                            and presentations
of brake linings and other automotive accessories, cardboard
displays, the dead roaming from one to another
as bored back in life as they are in hell, poor and doomed
to mere equipments

          my mother, as alive as ever she was, asleep
when I entered the house as I often found her in a rocker
under the lamp, and awaking, as I came up to her,
                          as she ever had

I found out she returns to the house once a week, and with her
the throng of the unknown young who center on her
                                  as much in death
as other like suited and dressed people did in life

O the dead!

        and the Indian woman and I
        enabled the blue deer
        to walk

        and the blue deer talked,
        in the next room,
        a Negro talk

        it was like walking a jackass,
        and its talk
        was the pressing gabber of gammers
        of old women

        and we helped walk it around the room
        because it was seeking socks
        or shoes for its hooves
        now that it was acquiring

        human possibilities

In the five hindrances men and angels
stay caught in the net, in the immense nets
which spread out across each plane of being, the multiple nets
which hamper at each step of the ladders as the angels
and the demons
and men
go up and down

            Walk the jackass
            Hear the victrola

Let the automobile
be tucked into a corner of the white fence
when it is a white chair. Purity

is only an instant of being, the trammels

recur

In the five hindrances, perfection
is hidden
                    I shall get
                    to the place
                    10 minutes late.

                    It will be 20 minutes
                    of 9. And I don't know,

                    without the car,

                    how I shall get there

O peace, my mother, I do not know
how differently I could have done
what I did or did not do.

                    That you are back each week
                    that you fall asleep
                    with your face to the right

                    that you are as present there
                    when I come in as you were
                    when you were alive

                    that you are as solid, and your flesh
                    is as I knew it, that you have the company
                    I am used to your having

but o, that you all find it
such a cheapness!

o peace, mother, for the mammothness
of the comings and goings
of the ladders of life

The nets we are entangled in. Awake,
my soul, let the power into the last wrinkle
of being, let none of the threads and rubber of the tires
be left upon the earth. Let even your mother
go. Let there be only paradise

The desperateness is, that the instant
which is also paradise (paradise
is happiness) dissolves
into the next instant, and power
flows to meet the next occurrence

                    Is it any wonder
                    my mother comes back?
                    Do not that throng
                    rightly seek the room
                    where they might expect
                    happiness? They did not complain
                    of life, they obviously wanted
                    the movie, each other, merely to pass
                    among each other there,
                    where the real is, even to the display cards,
                    to be out of hell

                    The poverty
                    of hell

O souls, in life and in death,
awake, even as you sleep, even in sleep
know what wind

even under the crankcase of the ugly automobile
lifts it away, clears the sodden weights of goods,
equipment, entertainment, the foods the Indian woman,
the filthy blue deer, the 4 by 3 foot 'Viewbook,'
the heaviness of the old house, the stuffed inner room
lifts the sodden nets

> and they disappear as ghosts do,
> as spider webs, nothing
> before the hand of man

> The vent! You must have the vent,
> or you shall die. Which means
> never to die, the ghastliness

> of going, and forever
> coming back, returning
> to the instants which were not lived

> O mother, this I could not have done,
> I could not have lived what you didn't,
> I am myself netted in my own being

> I want to die. I want to make that instant, too,
> perfect

> O my soul, slip
> the cog

II

The death in life (death itself)
is endless, eternity
is the false cause

The knot is otherwise, each topological corner
presents itself, and no sword
cuts it, each knot is itself its fire

each knot of which the net is made
is for the hands to untake
the knot's making. And touch alone

can turn the knot into its own flame

        (o mother, if you had once touched me

          o mother, if I had once touched you)

The car did not burn. Its underside
was not presented to me
a grotesque corpse. The old man

merely removed it as I looked up at it,
and put it in a corner of the picket fence
like was it my mother's white dog?

or a child's chair

        The woman,
        playing on the grass,
        with her son (the woman next door)

        was angry with me whatever it was
        slipped across the playpen or whatever
        she had out there on the grass

        And I was quite flip in reply
        that anyone who used plastic
        had to expect things to skid

        and break, that I couldn't worry
        that her son might have been hurt
        by whatever it was I sent skidding

        down on them.

It was just then I went into my house
and to my utter astonishment
found my mother sitting there

as she always had sat, as must she always
forever sit there her head lolling
into sleep? Awake, awake my mother

what wind will lift you too
forever from the tawdriness,
make you rich as all those souls

crave crave crave

to be rich?

They are right. We must have
what we want. We cannot afford
not to. We have only one course:

the nets which entangle us are flames

O souls, burn
alive, burn now

that you may forever
have peace, have

what you crave

O souls,
go into everything,
let not one knot pass
through your fingers

let not any they tell you
you must sleep as the net
comes through your authentic hands

What passes
is what is, what shall be, what has
been, what hell and heaven is
is earth to be rent, to shoot you
through the screen of flame which each knot
hides as all knots are a wall ready
to be shot open by you

                    the nets of being
are only eternal if you sleep as your hands
ought to be busy. Method, method

I too call on you to come
to the aid of all men, to women most
who know most, to woman to tell
men to awake. Awake, men,
awake

I ask my mother
to sleep. I ask her
to stay in the chair.
My chair
is in the corner of the fence.
She sits by the fireplace made of paving stones. The blue deer
need not trouble either of us.

And if she sits in happiness the souls
who trouble her and me
will also rest. The automobile

has been hauled away.

VARIATIONS DONE FOR
GERALD VAN DE WIELE

dogwood flakes
what is green

the petals
from the apple
blow on the road

mourning doves
mark the sway
of the afternoon, bees
dig the plum blossoms

the morning
stands up straight, the night
is blue from the full of the April moon

iris and lilac, birds
birds, yellow flowers
white flowers, the Diesel
does not let up dragging
the plow

      as the whippoorwill,
the night's tractor, grinds
his song

and no other birds but us
are as busy (O saisons, o chateaux!

Délires!

What soul
is without fault?

Nobody studies
happiness

Every time the cock crows
I salute him

I have no longer any excuse
for envy. My life

has been given its orders: the seasons
seize

the soul and the body, and make mock
of any dispersed effort. The hour of death

is the only trespass

II. THE CHARGE

dogwood flakes
the green

the petals from the apple-trees
fall for the feet to walk on

the birds are so many they are
loud, in the afternoon

they distract, as so many bees do
suddenly all over the place

With spring one knows today to see
that in the morning each thing

is separate but by noon
they have melted into each other

and by night only crazy things
like the full moon and the whippoorwill

and us, are busy. We are busy
if we can get by that whiskered bird,

that nightjar, and get across, the moon
is our conversation, she will say

what soul
isn't in default?

can you afford not to make
the magical study

which happiness is? do you hear
the cock when he crows? do you know the charge,

that you shall have no envy, that your life
has its orders, that the seasons

seize you too, that no body and soul are one
if they are not wrought

in this retort? that otherwise efforts
are efforts? And that the hour of your flight

will be the hour of your death?

The dogwood
lights up the day.

The April moon
flakes the night.

Birds, suddenly,
are a multitude

The flowers are ravined
by bees, the fruit blossoms

are thrown to the ground, the wind
the rain forces everything. Noise—

even the night is drummed
by whippoorwills, and we get

as busy, we plow, we move,
we break out, we love. The secret

which got lost neither hides
nor reveals itself, it shows forth

tokens. And we rush
to catch up. The body

whips the soul. In its great desire
it demands the elixir

In the roar of spring,
transmutations. Envy

drags herself off. The fault of the body and the soul
—that they are not one—

the matutinal cock clangs
and singleness: we salute you

season of no bungling

THE LIBRARIAN

The landscape (the landscape!) again: Gloucester,
the shore one of me is (duplicates), and from which
(from offshore, I, Maximus) am removed, observe.

In this night I moved on the territory with combinations
(new mixtures) of old and known personages: the leader,
my father, in an old guise, here selling books and manuscripts.

My thought was, as I looked in the window of his shop,
there should be materials here for Maximus, when, then,
I saw he was the young musician has been there (been before me)

before. It turned out it wasn't a shop, it was a loft (wharf-
house) in which, as he walked me around, a year ago
came back (I had been there before, with my wife and son,

I didn't remember, he presented me with insinuations via
himself and his girl) both of whom I had known for years.
But never in Gloucester. I had moved them in, to my country.

His previous appearance had been in my parents'
                                        bedroom where I
found him intimate with my former wife: this boy
was now the Librarian of Gloucester, Massachusetts!

     Black space,
     old fish-house.
     Motions
     of ghosts.

I,
dogging
his steps.

He
(not my father,
by name himself
with his face
twisted
at birth)
possessed of knowledge
pretentious
giving me
what in the instant
I knew better of.

But the somber
place, the flooring
crude like a wharf's
and a barn's
space

I was struck by the fact I was in Gloucester, and
that my daughter
was there—that I would see her! She was over the Cut. I
hadn't even connected her with my being there, that she was

here. That she was there (in the Promised Land—the Cut!
But there was this business, of poets, that all my Jews
were in the fish-house too, that the Librarian had made a party

I was to read. They were. There were many of them, slumped
around. It was not for me. I was outside. It was the Fort.
The Fort was in East Gloucester—old Gorton's Wharf,
where the Library

was. It was a region of coal houses, bins. In one a gang
was beating someone to death, in a corner of the labyrinth
of fences. I could see their arms and shoulders whacking

down. But not the victim. I got out of there. But cops
tailed me along the Fort beach toward the Tavern

The places still
half-dark, mud,
coal-dust.

There is no light
east
of the Bridge

Only on the headland
toward the harbor
from Cressy's

have I seen it (once
when my daughter ran
out on a spit of sand

isn't even there.) Where
is Bristow? when does I-A
get me home? I am caught

in Gloucester. (What's buried
behind Lufkin's
Diner? Who is

Frank Moore?

MOONSET, GLOUCESTER,
DECEMBER 1, 1957, 1:58 A.M.

Goodbye red moon
In that color you set
west of the Cut I should imagine
forever Mother

After 47 years this month
a Monday at 9 A.M.
you set I rise I hope
a free thing as probably
what you more were Not
the suffering one you sold
sowed me on Rise
Mother from off me
God damn you God damn me my
misunderstanding of you

I can die now I just begun to live

THE DISTANCES

So the distances are Galatea
                                and one does fall in love and desires
mastery

      old Zeus—young Augustus

Love knows no distance, no place
                                is that far away or heat changes
into signals, and control

      old Zeus—young Augustus

Death is a loving matter, then, a horror
                                we cannot bide, and avoid
by greedy life

      we think all living things are precious
      —Pygmalions

            a German inventor in Key West
who had a Cuban girl, and kept her, after her death
in his bed
                                after her family retrieved her
he stole the body again from the vault

Torso on torso in either direction,
      young Augustus
                                out via nothing where messages
are
   or in, down La Cluny's steps to the old man sitting
a god throned on torsoes,

      old Zeus

Sons go there hopefully as though there was a secret, the object
to undo distance?
                        They huddle there, at the bottom
of the shaft, against one young bum
                        or two loving cheeks,

        Augustus?

You can teach the young nothing
                        all of them go away, Aphrodite
tricks it out,
            old Zeus—young Augustus

You have love, and no object
                        or you have all pressed to your nose
which is too close,

            old Zeus hiding in your chin your young
            Galatea

the girl who makes you weep, and you keep the corpse live by all
your arts

            whose cheek do you stroke when you
                                stroke the stone face
            of young Augustus, made for bed in
                        a military camp, o Caesar?

O love who places all where each is, as they are, for every moment,
yield
            to this man
                        that the impossible distance
be healed,
            that young Augustus
            and old Zeus
be enclosed

        "I wake you,
stone. Love this man."

222

V

LETTER 3

Tansy buttons, tansy
for my city
Tansy for their noses

Tansy for them,
tansy for Gloucester to take the smell
of all owners,
the smell

Tansy
for all of us

    Let those who use words cheap, who use us cheap
    take themselves out of the way
    Let them not talk of what is good for the city

    Let them free the way for me, for the men of the Fort
    who are not hired, who buy the white houses

    Let them cease putting out words in the public print
    so that any of us have to leave, so that my Portuguese leave,
    leave the Lady they gave us, sell their schooners
    with the greyhounds aft, the long Diesels
    they put their money in, leave Gloucester
    in the present shame of,
    the wondership stolen by,
    ownership

Tansy from Cressy's
I rolled in as a boy

and didn't know it was
tansy

1

Did you know, she sd, growing up there,
how rare it was? And it turned out later she meant
                              exactly the long field
drops down from Ravenswood where the land abrupts,
this side of Fresh Water Cove, and throws out
that wonder of my childhood, the descending green does run
so,
by the beach

              where they held the muster Labor Day,
                              and the engine teams
              threw such arcs of water

                              runs with summer with
tansy

2

I was not born there, came, as so many of the people came,
from elsewhere. That is, my father did. And not
                              from the Provinces,
not from Newfoundland. But we came early enough.
                              When he came,
there were three hundred sail could fill the harbor,
if they were all in, as for the Races, say
Or as now the Italians are in, for San Pietro,
and the way it is from Town Landing, all band-concert,
and fireworks

So I answered her: Yes,
I knew (I had that to compare to it,
was Worcester)

As the people of the earth are now, Gloucester
is heterogeneous, and so can know polis
not as localism, not that mu-sick (the trick
of corporations, newspapers, slick magazines, movie houses,
the ships, even the wharves, absentee-owned

they whine to my people, these entertainers, sellers

they play upon their bigotries (upon their fears

these   they have the nerve
to speak of that lovely hour
the Waiting Station, 5 o'clock, the Magnolia bus, Al Levy
on duty (the difference
from 1 o'clock, all the women getting off
the Annisquam-Lanesville,
and the letter carriers

5:40, and only the lollers
in front of the shoe-shine parlor

these, right in the people's faces (and not at all as the gulls do it,
who do it straight, do it all over the "Times" blowing
the day after, or the "Summer Sun" catching on pilings, floating
off the Landing, the slime
the low tide reveals, the smell
then

3

The word does intimidate. The pay-check does.
But to use either, as cheap men

o tansy city, root city
let them not make you
as the nation is

I speak to any of you, not to you all, to no group,
                              nor to you as citizens
as my Tyrian might have. Polis now
is a few, is a coherence not even yet new (the island of this city
is a mainland now of who? who can say who are
citizens?

Only a man or a girl who hear a word
and that word meant to mean not a single thing
                              the least more than
what it does mean (not at all to sell any one anything,
                              to keep them anywhere,
not even
in this rare place

        Root person in root place, hear one tansy-covered
                              boy tell you
what any knowing man of your city might, a letter carrier, say,
or that doctor—if they dared afford to take the risk,
                              if they reminded themselves
that you should not be played with, that you deserve . . .
                              they'd tell you
the condition of the under-water, the cut-water
                              of anyone, including those
who take on themselves
to give you advice,
to tell you, for example,
what not to read

        They'd tell you, because they know (know
                              as the house knows,
wearing its white face, its clapboard mask) who there is
                              will not outrage you
in the next edition, who'll not seek, even knowingly, to make you
slave

as he is slave
whom you read
as the bus starts off

whose slaver
would keep you off the sea, would keep you local,
my Nova Scotians,
Newfoundlanders,
Sicilianos,
Isolatos

4

Isolated person in Gloucester, Massachusetts, I, Maximus,
address you
you islands
of men and girls

THE SONGS OF MAXIMUS

Song 1

       colored pictures
of all things to eat: dirty
postcards
         And words, words, words
all over everything
              No eyes or ears left
to do their own doings (all

invaded, appropriated, outraged, all senses

including the mind, that worker on what is
                  And that other sense
made to give even the most wretched, or any of us, wretched,
that consolation (greased
             lulled
even the street-cars

song

Song 2

     all
wrong
       And I am asked—ask myself (I, too, covered
with the gurry of it) where
shall we go from here, what can we do
when even the public conveyances
sing?
       how can we go anywhere,

even cross-town
                    how get out of anywhere (the bodies
all buried
in shallow graves?

SONG 3

        This morning of the small snow
I count the blessings, the leak in the faucet
which makes of the sink time, the drop
of the water on water as sweet
as the Seth Thomas
in the old kitchen
my father stood in his drawers to wind (always
he forgot the 30th day, as I don't want to remember
the rent
            a house these days
so much somebody else's,
especially,
Congoleum's

            Or the plumbing,
that it doesn't work, this I like, have even used paper clips
as well as string to hold the ball up And flush it
with my hand
            But that the car doesn't, that no moving thing moves
without that song I'd void my ear of, the musickracket
of all ownership . . .
                    Holes
in my shoes, that's all right, my fly
gaping, me out
at the elbows, the blessing
                    that difficulties are once more

        "In the midst of plenty, walk
        as close to
        bare

In the face of sweetness,
piss
                    In the time of goodness,
go side, go
smashing, beat them, go as
(as near as you can

tear

In the land of plenty, have
nothing to do with it
                    take the way of
the lowest,
including
your legs, go
contrary, go

sing

Song 4

I know a house made of mud & wattles,
I know a dress just sewed
                    (saw the wind
blow its cotton
against her body
from the ankle
                    so!
it was Nike

                    And her feet: such bones
I could have had the tears
that lovely pedant had
who couldn't unwrap it himself, had to ask them to,
                              on the schooner's deck

and he looked,
the first human eyes to look again

at the start of human motion (just last week
300,000,000 years ago

                    She
was going fast
across the square, the water
this time of year, that
scarce

And the fish

Song 5

I have seen faces of want,
and have not wanted the FAO: Appleseed
's gone back to
what any of us
New England

Song 6

you sing, you

who also

wants

LETTER 6

polis is
eyes

> (Moulton cried up that day,
> "Where'd you get those glasses?"
> after, like a greenhorn,
> I'd picked three swordfish out of the sun-blaze
> where no regular could afford to look,
> to waste his eyes seeking a fin in that place

I have suffered since,
from that enthusiasm

> as my heart has never been so good
> as the day I'd be damned if that Englishman,
> and mountain-climber,
> would beat me
> up the Bright Angel trail
>   I'd been the cannier
> in the descent, had a chocolate bar we all ate
> as we cooled our feet in the Colorado
>   It was coming up
> I spent myself, falling face-flat each step I managed,
> flopping in the fine dust which mules,
> wiser & wealthier persons rode,
> had ground the sandstone to)

It is just such folly is not necessary, yet I have not noticed
that those who are sharp haven't got that way
by pushing their limits

                    (above me,
when Moulton hollered from the wheel,
was Burke, humped over the masthead like the ball
on top of a weather-pole, he squatting in the canvas strap,
the rest of us standing in the whale-rope rigging, all of us
like birds in a cote, and he the leader
as he well was, he was that good a professional, his eyes
as a gull's are, or any Portygee's,
and the long visor of his cap more of a beak
than even the same we all wore

It is of the matter that this Burke on land was a drunk
                              (though, one Sunday,
I did see him on the wharf with his kids, showing them
                                    the vessel, he
in a blue suit, and the old stiff straw, the only time
                                I did see him so,
like the oval portrait hangs
in so many living rooms
                    not at all the same grace of a man
came up on deck at sea in oilskins (as Olsen,
                    two days out, would appear
in a new white shirt and new fedora, Hyperion
to the lump his men would have wheeled aboard,
at sailing time,
in a barrow)

It makes sense that these men

            Burke was raising his family
            in a shack out over the marsh;
            and Olsen, they now tell me,
            is carting fish, for Gorton-Pew,
            the lowest job, Gloucester,
            the job we all started with

            young Douglas, who never went to sea,
            he's different, is in the front office

at Gorton-Pew, was so good a ball player
he got moved up, and fast:

he gave me cans of cooked mackerel,
the last time I was home, "for the ride back"
he said, and I couldn't tell him I hate
picnics
           ("pick-nicks," Pound roared
when Con suggested we have fried chicken,
and get him out of S'Liz for the afternoon,
eat alongside the tennis courts
out over the Anacostia
                     I was against it
for another reason, because of the Navy planes
roar in just there, and the chatter of the patients
was more to my liking as background
for the great man, in his black coat and wide hat,
                            the whole man
wagging, the swag
of Pound

Eyes,
& polis,
fishermen,
& poets
        or in every human head I've known is
        busy
both:
the attention, and
the care
        however much each of us
        chooses our own
        kin and
        concentration

2

And the few—that goes, even inside the major
economics. It is not true that the many,
even in fishing, say, Gloucester,
are the gauge
            (where Ferrini, as so many,
            go wrong
so few
have the polis
in their eye
            The brilliant Portuguese owners,
            they do. They pour the money back
            into engines, into their ships,
            whole families do, put it back
            in. They are but extensions of their own careers
            as mastheadsmen—as Burkes

(the day we all stood around on the wharf examining the Laura
Dysart, the gash in her bow, and her foremast snapped off, where
the Magellan had piled into her. And Dysart himself telling
about it, the thing still right in front of him, how neither he
nor Captain Rose would give way, both of them coming up on
the same fish. What struck me was, Dysart's admiration, how
the Magellan had overtaken him, from the speed of her Diesels,
and he saying he was sure Rose had sighted the fish as soon as
he had, aft of him though she was, those island eyes that very
damned good, and he, Dysart, and his ship, witness to it

So few need to,
to make the many
share (to have it,
too)

but those few . . .

What kills me is, how do these others think
the eyes are
sharp? by gift? bah   by love of self? try it   by god? ask
the bean sandwich

There are no hierarchies, no infinite,
                            no such many as mass, there are only
eyes in all heads,
to be looked out of

TYRIAN BUSINESSES

1

The waist of a lion,
for a man to move properly

And for a woman,
who should move lazily,
the weight of breasts

This is the exercise for this morning

2

how to dance
sitting down

3

or the one so far back she craves to be scalped,
and dragged over the ground
                    And because nobody has dragged her,
she has everybody do it. She does it. She wants clean sheets,
each night
                    as that other, that international doll,
has to have silk, when she is put up
                              (why is she put up with?)
in the white house

4

Or there are those sing ditties, that dead reason
of personality, the will of, like a seal
of a mealy justice: the body a shell, the mind also
an apparatus

There are so many, children,
who want to go back, who want to lie down
in Tiamat. They sing:
euphoria

5

You can tell them this: the land-spout's
put all the diapers
up in trees (what musicians call
the middle voice, to command it
is to be in business.
            There may be no more names than there are objects
            There can be no more verbs than there are actions

It is still
morning

II

a hollow muscular organ which, by contracting vigorously,
                                            keeps up the

        (to have the heart

                (a whorl of green bracts at the base

                                                    (ling,

she is known as

        Weather
comes generally
        under the
            metaphrast.

                    (when M is above G, all's
                    well. When below, there's
                    upset. When M and G are coincident,
                    it is not very interesting)

1

        (peltate
is my nose-twist, my beloved, my
trophy
            tropical American diffuse and climbing pungent
            with lobed or dissected
            And showy, e.g. so variously colored,
                            a garden species, the

2

totipalmate
is the toc And so vain
it plucks its tail to free the handsome green eye from
redundant feathers Which, then, it switches
to admire itself, as any Egyptian lady
must have looked fixing herself
by polished stone
            (The farmer whose nephew we knew
was so exasperated
he used to heave anything at the bird, swearing
if his face got reflected in that burnished tail
he'd die,
right then & there

3

The seedling
of morning: to move, the problems (after the night's presences)
                    the first hours of

      He had noticed,
      the cotton picks easiest

          As my flower,
          after rain, wears
          such diadem

As a man is a necklace
strung of his own teeth (the caries
of 'em

He sd: Notice
the whiteness, not
the odor of
the dead night

4

(the honey in the lion, the honey
in woman

5

"felicity
resulting from life of activity in accordance with"

Which is the question: in accordance with what?

Ukase: "the vertical
        through the center of buoyancy of a
floating body
        intersects
the vertical through the new
center made . . .

when the wind,

or the nature of the cargo

or a rip

        (so much it was the rain and the wind when we were
running to eastward before it. I had stood the third watch, and
when I came below they say I was that pale. For cause: the
lightning had stepped along the sea straight at us, so that I at
the wheel could calculate whether the next one would hit us
fore, or aft, or strike us amidships.

For three days the glass had read 29.2, and we had, you might say, eat our cigarettes, there seemed no reason to think the "Hawes" would weather that one, she being so small, and her screws no damned good anyway. Moulton had been that greedy, he wanted to pick up all the lumber we see floating ahead of us on the sea, had broke off the deck of some schooner had lost her lashings. For the garage he was building, Rockport.

It was crazy, coming up on those dead sticks cross-wise in the seas, not at all like coming up on those fish would scare the moment the iron, or the shadow of it, came at them. Or, once hit, how they'd run for it. And any of us, out over into a dory to battle them, for how many hours, alone, on the sea.

This, was no game at all, though none of us thought of the danger, even the skipper himself. He just wanted this windfall, and he ordered the striker out on the pulpit and the rest of us along the starboard side, the usual side to take up the slack of the line when the sword was making his first run away with it.

We gaffed a half a dozen of those planks, and it was party stuff—even the cook had gone below, he was so bored, was in the galley when it happened, told us afterward how it sounded, there. What happened was, Moulton fetched the vessel straight on one plank plunk in its middle, and it stayed there, right in its center, even when it swayed below water: you could hear it passing the length of the keel, bumping, bumping, but never losing, from the forward speed of the vessel, the center of her Moulton had hit her by.

Then there was the noise—and the ship suddenly acting as no ship ever did, as the blades of the screw bit into that wood, and as that wood chewed them up!

We watched the mess of it astern going off in the wake as the vessel fell off so she felt like dead in the water.

It was a caution, the rest of that trip was—63 fish, and most of them babies. And a lot of the big ones spoiled, we had to stay out so long to try to make up for our losses, not just to the fast Portygees, but to any schooner of the swordfishing fleet that July. Even the Little David, out of Edgartown, could get there ahead of us.

We were five weeks, from Moulton's folly— and that storm drove us four days before it, trying to get out of its path. The whole fleet scattered, but we had the worst of it, from no power. The last week, we had to have cod to eat, from Olsen's Raymonde, he roaring, in that voice of his, "Come aboard, Cece—come aboard, and get some cod!", it sounding, over the water, like the barrel of god.

I rowed the skipper over.

6

Definition: (in this instance, and in what others, what felicities?

"The crooked timbers scarfed together to form the lower part of the compound rib are

futtocks, we call 'em

But a fylfot, she look like, who calls herself

(luck

MAXIMUS, TO HIMSELF

I have had to learn the simplest things
last. Which made for difficulties.
Even at sea I was slow, to get the hand out, or to cross
a wet deck.
                    The sea was not, finally, my trade.
But even my trade, at it, I stood estranged
from that which was most familiar. Was delayed,
and not content with the man's argument
that such postponement
is now the nature of
obedience,
                    that we are all late
                    in a slow time,
                    that we grow up many
                    And the single
                    is not easily
                    known

It could be, though the sharpness (the *achiote*)
I note in others,
makes more sense
than my own distances. The agilities

                    they show daily
                    who do the world's
                    businesses
                    And who do nature's
                    as I have no sense
                    I have done either

I have made dialogues,
have discussed ancient texts,
have thrown what light I could, offered
what pleasures
doceat allows

But the known?
This, I have had to be given,
a life, love, and from one man
the world.

Tokens.
But sitting here
I look out as a wind
and water man, testing
And missing
some proof

I know the quarters
of the weather, where it comes from,
where it goes. But the stem of me,
this I took from their welcome,
or their rejection, of me

And my arrogance
was neither diminished
nor increased,
by the communication

2

It is undone business
I speak of, this morning,
with the sea
stretching out
from my feet

MAXIMUS, TO GLOUCESTER

It goes to show you. It was not the "Eppie Sawyer." It was the ship "Putnam." It wasn't Christmas morning, it was Christmas night, after dark. And the violent north-easter, with snow, which we were all raised to believe did show Bowditch such a navigator, was a gale sprung up from W, hit them outside the Bay, and had blown itself out by the 23rd.

On the 25th it was fog Bowditch had to contend with. The wind was NE allright, but there is no mention of snow. At 4 P.M. it cleared a little and he was able to see Eastern Point. And at 7 he came to anchor in Salem. In other words it was the beacon at Gloucester, not the light on Baker's Island—there was no light on Eastern Point until 1831—which got him home.

The whole tale, as we have had it, from his son, goes by the board. The son seems to have got it thirty-five years after the event from a sailor who was with the father on that voyage (to Sumatra, and Ile de France, cargo: shoes). This sailor apparently (he was twenty years older than the captain) was the one who said, that night they did get in, "Our old man goes ahead as if it was noonday." He must have been 85 when he added the rest of the tale—how the owners were very much alarmed at Bowditch's sudden appearance "on such a tempestuous night," and how, at first, they could hardly be persuaded he had not been wrecked.

1

He sd, "You go all around the subject." And I sd, "I didn't know it was a subject." He sd, "You twist" and I sd, "I do." He said other things. And I didn't say anything.

Nor do I know

that this is a rail

on which all (or any)

will ride (as, by Pullman

that sense the ads are right abt, that you are

taken care of, you do

not sleep, you are

jolted

And if you take a compartment,

the whole damned family . . .

I sd, "Rhapsodia . . .

II

John Smith's latest book was,
"ADVERTISEMENTS
for the unexperienced Planters
of New-England,

        or anywhere" (dedicated
        to the Archbishops of Canterbury,
        and York, primates,
        it says,
        of England (1630)

The epigraph
is a poem
by sd Smith (refused

as navigator by
the Pilgrims, Standish
chosen instead)

THE SEA MARKE

It reads (Smith died,

that year):

"Aloofe, aloofe; and come no neare,
      the dangers doe appeare;
Which if my ruine had not beene
      you had not seene:
I onely lie upon this shelfe
      to be a marke to all
      which on the same might fall,
That none may perish but my selfe.

    "If in or outward you be bound,
        do not forget to sound;
    Neglect of that was cause of this
        to steere amisse:
    The Seas were calme, the wind was faire,
        that made me so secure,
        that now I must indure
    All weathers be they foule or faire

        "The Winters cold, the Summers heat
            alternatively beat

Upon my bruised sides, that rue
because too true
That no releefe can ever come.
But why should I despaire
being promised so faire
That there shall be a day of Dome"

III

And for the water-shed, the economics & poetics thereafter?

Three men,

coincide:

    you will find Villon
in Fra Diavolo,
Elberthubbardsville,
N. Y.

    And the prose
is Raymond's, Boston, or
Brer Fox,
Rapallo,
Quattrocento-by-the-Beach, #
429

    The American epos, 19-

02 (or when did Barton Barton Barton Barton and Barton?

To celebrate

how it can be, it is

padded or uncomforted, your lost, you

found, your

sneakers

(o Statue,
o Republic, o
Tell-A-Vision, the best
is soap. The true troubadours
are CBS. Melopoeia

is for Cokes by Cokes out of

Pause

IV

(o Po-ets, you

should getta

job

ON FIRST LOOKING OUT
THROUGH JUAN DE LA
COSA'S EYES

> Behaim—and nothing
> insula Azores to
> Cipangu (Candyn
> somewhere also there where spices
>
> and yes, in the Atlantic,
> one floating island: de
> Sant
>   brand
>   an

1

St Malo, however.
Or Biscay. Or Bristol.
Fishermen, had,
for how long,
talked:
      Heavy sea,
snow, hail. At 8
A.M. a tide rip. Sounded.
Had 20 fath. decreased from that to
15, 10. Wore ship.

    (They knew
Cap Raz

(As men, my town, my two towns
talk, talked of Gades, talk
of Cash's

drew, on a table, in spelt,
with a finger, in beer, a
portulans

> But before La Cosa, nobody
> could have
> a mappemunde

2

(What he drew who drew Hercules
going by the Bear off from Calypso

Now, it would be breakers, Sable!
ahead, where, just off,
you could put buckets down

> (You could go any coast
> in such a raft as she taught,
> as she taught him, favoring him

with cedar, & much niceties. It was only because the gods willed
that he could leave her, go away, determined
though he had been the whole time
not to eat her food, not to wear gods' clothes,
to stick to what men eat

And wore

> The Atlantic,
> just then,
> was to take kings,
> & fishermen

And Europe,
was being drained
of gold

II

but cod? The New Land was,
from the start, even by name was
Bacalhaos
            there,
swimming, Norte, out of the mists

                    (out of Pytheus' sludge

out of mermaids & Monsters

                    (out of Judas-land

Tierra,
de bacalaos, out of

waters   Massachusetts,
                    my Newfoundlanders
                    My Portuguese: you

(Or Verrazano has it,
curiously, put down as
a Mud Bank

                    "Sounding
                    on George's
                    25 fath. sand. At the same time spoke
                    the Brig Albion, Packet,
                    John Dogget who told us
                    Cape Ann was 80 leag.
                    dis.

Terra nova sive Limo Lue,
he wrote it who knew it
as only Corte Real   (the first known lost
as Bertomez (as Cabot?

> Who found you,
>
> land,
>
> of the hard gale?

1

Respecting the earth, he sd,
it is a pear, or,
like a round ball upon a part of which there is a prominence
like a woman's nipple, this protrusion
is the highest & nearest to
the sky

   Ships
have always represented a large capital investment,
           and the manning,
the provisioning of same

        It was the teredo-worm
        was 1492: riddle a ship's hull
        in one voyage ("pierced
with worm-holes
like a bee-hive,
the report was

        Ladies & Gentlemen,
        he lost his pearl,
        he lost the Indies
        to a worm

2

North? Mud. 1480 John Lloyd, the most expert shipmaster
              of all England,

on behalf of John Jay and other merchants Bristol
set out to
the island of Brasylle, to
traverse the seas

Nine weeks. And storms
threw him back.
     No worms. Storms,
     Ladies &

     to the bottom of the,

     husbands, & wives,

     little children lost their

(4,670 fishermen's lives are noticed. In an outgoing tide
of the Annisquam River, each summer, at the August full,
they throw flowers, which, from the current there, at the Cut,
reach the harbor channel, and go

these bouquets (there are few, Gloucester, who can
          afford florists' prices)
float out
     you can watch them go out into,
the Atlantic

III

On ne doit aux morts nothing

   else than

la vérité

THE TWIST

Trolley-cars
are my inland waters
(Tatnuck Sq, and the walk
 from the end of the line
 to Paxton, for May-flowers

 or by the old road to Holden,
 after English walnuts

And my wife has a new baby
in a house at the end of
such a line, and the morning after,
is ready to come home, the baby too,
exceptionally well & advanced

Or he and I distinguish
between chanting,
and letting the song lie
in the thing itself.
I plant flowers
(xenia) for him,
in the wet soil, indoors,
in his house

As I had it in my first poem,
the Annisquam
fills itself, at its tides, as she did
the French dress, cut
on the bias,

my neap,
my spring-tide, my
waters

1

Between Newton and Tatnuck Square the tracks
go up hill, the cars
sway, as they go around the bend
before they take, before they go down to
the outer-land
(where it is Sunday,
   I am small, people go off
   what strikes me as questionable
   directions. They are large,
   going away from my father and me,
   as cows on that landscape

   he and I seeming
   the only ones who know
   what we are doing, where
   we are going

Now I find out it is the Severn
goes from Worcester to Gloucester to
: Bristow, Smith called it,
what sticks in me as the promised land
those couples did go to, at right angles
from us, what does show
between Gloucester and Boston, the landscape
I go up-dilly, elevated, tenement
down

2

It rained,
the day we arrived.
And I have rowed the harbor since,

out the window of Johnny's Candy Kitchen,
through that glass and rain through which I looked
the first time I saw
the sea.

    She was staying,
after she left me,
in an apartment house
was like cake

        When I found her
—the people in it like Macomber
who lived under me on Charles St—next door
a man in a bowler hat scutted away,
the same man had fired a bullet
into her ho-ho

       Or it was Schwartz,
the bookie, whose mother-in-law
I'd have gladly gone to bed with

    Her room (the house
was a *dobostorte*), the door
high up on the wall,
#48,
small,
like an oven-door

The harbor the same,
the night of the St Valentine
storm: the air
sea   ground   the same, tossed
ice   wind   snow   (Pytheus) one

       cakes falling
as quiet as I was

out of the sky as quiet
as the blizzard was

3

When I woke
in the toy house I had headed for, the look
out my window
sent me, the whiteness
in the morning sun, the figures

shoveling

     I went home
as fast as I could,

the whole Cut
was a paper village my Aunt Vandla
had given me, who gave me,
each Christmas,
such toys

As dreams are, when the day
encompasses. They tear down
the Third Ave El.   Mine stays,
as Boston does, inches up.
I run my trains
on a monorail, I am seized
—not so many nights ago—
by the sight of the river
exactly there at the Bridge

where it goes out & in

I recognize
the country not discovera,
the marsh behind, the ditch that Blynman made, the dog-rocks
the tide roars over

>   some curves off,
> when it's the river's turn, shoots
> calyx and corolla by the dog
>   (August,
> the flowers break off

>   but the anther,
> the filament of now, the mass
> drives on,

>   the whole of it
> coming,
> to this pin-point
> to turn

>   in this day's sun,

> in this veracity

> there, the waters the several of them the roads

> here, a blackberry blossom

LETTER 22

> (Trouble
> with the car. And for a buck
> they gave me
> what I found myself
> eating! A polishing
> cloth. And I went right on
> eating it, it was that good.
> And thick, color
> orange & black, with a nap—the billowing dress
> the big girl wears
> every so often

1

What weeds
as an explanation
leaves out, is
that chaos
is not our condition.

Not that relaxation.

                    All,
has no honor as quantity.

        And the attention,
in each of us,
is that one, not the other
not the perfect one. Beauty,
is too quick
for time

If man is omnivore,
and he is, he eats anything
every so often, he is also
amorvore
as well

                    (She lost her finger.
                    And the problem was,
                    at the celebration,
                    where to seat the
                    stranger:
                            Goomeranian,
                    his name was.
                            And he wore
                    a big smile

2

"Satie, enough"

was what it said

                Satie,

enough

And I wear it,

as my blazon

                moving

among my particulars, among

my foes

264

3

And what I write
is stopping the battle,

to get down, right in the midst of
the deeds, to tell

what this one did, how,
in the fray, he made this play, did grapple
with that one, how
his eye flashed

        to celebrate

(beauty will not wait)

men,

and girls

        (I swung the car to the left, confronted
        as I was by the whole hill-front
        a loading platform, the lip of it
        staring at me, grinning,
        you might say,
        five feet off
        the ground

        And made it. It was only after
        that the car gave me
        trouble.

        For there is a limit
        to what a car
        will do.

SOME GOOD NEWS

how small the news was
a permanent change had come
by 14 men setting down
on Cape Ann, on the westerly side
of the harbor

        the same side Bradford,
the fall before, had asked London
to get for him
so that New Plymouth
could prosecute fishing, no place,

in the minds of men, England
or on the ground, equal,
and fitting the future
as this Cape sitting
between the old

North Atlantic (of Biskay,
and Breton, of Cabot's
nosing into, for Bristol)
and the new—Georges
(as the bank was called as early

as 1530: who gave her their
patron saint—England?
Aragon? or Portyngales?)
Or Old Man's Pasture, Tillies
Bank, whichever way

you take what advantage
Cape Ann: Levett

says "too faire a gloss"
is placed on her,
the same year

New Plymouth here,
Dorchester there,
and Levett himself,
at Quack, care
to be right. 1623,

all of them,
suddenly,
pay attention,
to what fishermen
(since when? before
1500) have

been showing: the motion
(the Westward motion)
comes here,
to land. Stations
(going back to sheep,
and goats on Sable

Island, of all sand spits
upon the globe, and terror
of blown or dragged or dropped
earth in the midst of
water—shoals, worse

than rock because
they do blow shift lie,
are changing as you sound—
on this crooked sand
Portuguese (when?)

had a fishing station.
It wasn't new,
what happened,

at Cape Ann. It's where,
and when it

did. Smith,
at Monhegan,
1614, and telling
about it, in a book,
1616, is

the demarcation (he,
the Sea-Marke!
as competently Columbus
backwards as Grant
forward, John Smith

the stater of
quantity and
precision, the double
doesn't unravel
so you'd know it

just like that, dragging,
as we do
shifty new
land, sucks
down, into the terrible

inert of
nature (the Divine
Inert, the literary man
of these men
of the West,

who knew private
passivity as these
quartermasters knew
supplies, said
it has to be

if princes
of the husting
are to issue from
the collapse
of the previous

soul: Smith,
too early yet
to be understood
to be the sign
of present

paternities—braggart
fishermen, the
Androgyne who hates
the simulacrum
Time Magazine

takes for male,
the playing coy
with identity)
a man's
struggle

with Caesar's
dream,
that he'd been intimate
with his mother,
and the soothsayer

eased him: it only means
that you shall conquer
the world. Smith,
as Sam Grant after,
was futile

until the place
and time burned
with the same heat as

the man (it isn't
for us to say

what a proper fire
is, it's what,
like Corinth
burning down
produces bronze—

or my Cabbage, we
baked potatoes
Fisher's Hill—or Caesar
dreamed, in Spain—or Smith,
who came to Monhegan

to catch whales,
found cod, instead.
And furs. And Frenchmen
ahead of him, west
of him. Yet

Smith
changed
everything: he pointed
out
Cape Ann,

named her
so it's stuck,
and Englishmen,
who were the ones
who wanted to,

sat down, planted
fisheries
so they've stayed put,
on this coast, from Pemaquid
to Cape Cod.

One needs
grab hold of,
with purchase
this purpose, that
the Continental Shelf

was Europe's
first West, it wasn't
Spain's
south: fish,
and furs

and timber,
were wealth,
neither plants,
old agricultural
growing, from

Neolithic, sickles
& that kind of
contemplation
of nature, she
the brooder

nor gold, and murder.
We kill
as a fisherman's
knife nicks
abundance.

Which we take
for granted,
we don't even earn
our labor (as patriarchy
and matriarchy)

we do it all
by quantity and
machine. The subjective

hides, or runs riot
("vainglorious,"

they put Smith down
as, and hire a Standish
to do corporative
murder: keep things clean,
by campaigns

drop bombs. One cries Mongols
instead. Yet Grant

still is a name
for butcher, for how
he did finally hammer out
a victory over

Clotho Lee, the spinner
the stocking frame
undid: textile
us, South
and North—the world,

tomorrow, and all
without fate
tomorrow,
if we,
who come from a housekeeping

which old mother Smith
started,
don't find out the inert
is as gleaming as,
and as fat as,

fish—so
we move: sd the
literary man, from hidden places

sprang
the killer's
instrument

who is also
the boatsteerer.
The "lily-iron,"
they called the swordfish
harpoon when Gloucester

still chased
the blue-backed
thing on Browns (east
of Monhegan, north
of Georges

   West
and south Smith
put down the claim;
and wrote
her paper
and her name

"The which
is riches
will change
the world" not knowing,
as we don't,

he'd hang up,
and be
a mark for all
who on this coast
do fall,

aloof aloof,
and come no near,

we cry. Or we'll over,
and you better
follow us who

from the hustings ("trash,"
industrial fish
are called which Gloucester
now catches, all that the bottom
of Georges,

the Channel, Middle Ground,
Browns, Pollock Rip
yields, anything
nature puts in the sea
comes up,

it is cornucopia
to see it
working up a sluggish
treadle,
from a ship's hold

to the truck
which takes it to the De-Hy
to be turned into catfood,
and fertilizer, for nature's
fields

Out of these waters
inland, it went. From then
—from Smith—some good news
better
get after

MAXIMUS, TO GLOUCESTER, SUNDAY, JULY 19

and they stopped before that bad sculpture of a fisherman

—"as if one were to talk to a man's house,
knowing not what gods or heroes are"—

not knowing what a fisherman is
instead of going straight to the Bridge
and doing no more than—saying no more than—
in the Charybdises of the
Cut waters the flowers tear off
the wreathes

the flowers
turn
the character of the sea   The sea jumps
the fate of the flower   The drowned men are undrowned
in the eddies
                of the eyes
                of the flowers
                opening
                the sea's eyes

The disaster
is undone
What was received as alien
—the flower
on the water, that a man drowns

that he dies in water as he dies on earth, the impossible
 that this gross fact can return to us
 in this upset
on a summer day
of a particular tide

that the sensation is true,
that the transformations of fire are, first of all, sea—
 "as gold for wares wares for gold"

 Let them be told who stopped first
 by a bronze idol

 A fisherman is not a successful man
 he is not a famous man he is not a man
 of power, these are the damned by God

II

whose surface bubbles
with these gimlets
which screw-in like

potholes, caustic
caked earth of painted
pools, Yellowstone

Park of holes
is death the diseased
presence on us, the spilling lesion

of the brilliance
it is to be alive: to walk onto it,
as Jim Bridger the first into it,

it is more true a scabious
field than it is a pretty
meadow

When a man's coffin is the sea
the whole of creation shall come to his funeral,

it turns out; the globe
is below, all lapis

and its blue surface golded
by what happened

this afternoon: there are eyes
in this water

the flowers
from the shore,

awakened
the sea

Men are so sure they know very many things,
they don't even know night and day are one

A fisherman works without reference to
that difference. It is possible he also

by lying there when he does lie, jowl
to the sea, has another advantage: it is said,

"You rectify what can be rectified," and when a man's heart
cannot see this, the door of his divine intelligence is shut

let you who paraded to the Cut today
to hold memorial services to all fishermen
who have been lost at sea in a year
when for the first time not one life was lost

radar sonar radio telephone good engines
bed-check seaplanes goodness over and under us

no difference
when men come back

BIBLIOGRAPHY

Call Me Ishmael. New York, 1947.

Upon a Moebus Strip. New York, 1947.

Portfolio V. Paris, 1947.

y & x. With drawings by Corrado Cagli. Paris, 1948.

The Sutter-Marshall Lease with the Yalesumney Indians for Monopoly of the Gold-Bearing Lands. (Introductory Notes by Charles Olson.) California, 1948.

Letter for Melville. Black Mountain, N.C., 1951.

Apollonius of Tyana. Black Mountain, N.C., 1952.

This. Black Mountain, N.C., 1952.

In Cold Hell, In Thicket. Mallorca, 1953.

Mayan Letters. Mallorca, 1953. Preface by Robert Creeley.

Maximus Poems / 1-10. Highlands, N.C., 1953.

Anecdotes of the Late War. Highlands, N.C., (1956).

Maximus Poems / 11-22. Highlands, N.C., 1956.

O'Ryan 2, 4, 6, 8, 10. San Francisco, 1958.

Projective Verse Vs. the Non-Projective. New York, 1959.

The Maximus Poems. New York, 1960.

The Distances. New York, 1960.

Maximus from Dogtown I. San Francisco, 1961. Foreword by Michael McClure.

A Bibliography on America for Ed Dorn. San Francisco, 1964.

Signature to Petition. Berkeley, 1964.

Human Universe and Other Essays. Edited by Donald Allen. San Francisco, 1965.

O'Ryan 1-10. San Francisco, 1965.

Proprioception. San Francisco, 1965.

*   *   *

There is never an end to such a selection as this, and I might well begin again, all over, making a very different choice. But I would, more usefully, invite the reader to that possibility. For example, he will want to read *Call Me Ishmael*, a book so integrated in its writing that I felt no excerpt was possible. Equally, he cannot accept what is here included from the *Maximus Poems* as in any sense the range of experience they undertake. They are a *continuing* work and the next volume, soon to be published, alters all sense of their conclusion.

Too, I should like to note the senses of other men which have been most valuable to me; more precisely, two works of exceptional critical reading:

Edward Dorn, *What I See In The Maximus Poems* (*Migrant*, 1960; reprinted *Kulchur* 4, 1961)

Robert Duncan, *Notes on Poetics Regarding Olson's "Maximus"* (*The Black Mountain Review* 6, 1956; reprinted and revised *The Review* 10, 1964)

I share deeply with both the occasion of what I have done.

R.C.